A
LEADER
PROVIDES

A
LEADER
PROVIDES

**OVER 200 YEARS OF MARINE
LEADERSHIP SKILLS, TACTICS
AND CODES FOR SUCCEEDING
IN BUSINESS AND IN LIFE**

Ernest R. Twigg and Robert S. Nahas

A LEADER PROVIDES

Editing and Layout by Robert S. Nahas of WriterServices.net

Writing Assistance by Russell Roberts of WriterServices.net

Cover and Ernest R. Twigg bio photos courtesy of John Cassevah at JRC Photography

Cover Design by Molly Courtright of WriterServices.net

Proofreading by Don Dewsnap of WriterServices.net

ISBN-10: 0-9800705-1-1
ISBN-13: 978-0-9800705-1-4

1. Self: Self-help, Self-Growth, Motivational, Experiences; **2. Business & Finance:** Leadership, Career, Employment, Strategic Planning, Finance/Money; **3. General Interest:** Inspirational

Published by:

 **PROMINENT BOOKS**™

Printed and bound in the U.S.A.

Prominent Books and the sunburst compass logo are Trademarks of Prominent Books, LLC

Table of Contents

◄◊► Dedication ◄◊►

This book is dedicated to my lovely wife, Katherine, for believing in me and keeping me on track, my magical daughter, Samantha, for restoring my belief, and to my father, Ernest, for instilling my moral compass.

‹◊›Acknowledgments‹◊›

Very special thanks to Robert S. Nahas for his writing work and editorial input with this book. His insight about the written word and ability to take so many of my ideas and concepts and make them palatable and well–understood was invaluable.

First Sergeant Edens- "Leaders do not flock; they are found one at a time."

Captain Barnhart- "It is not just about winning, it's all about winning!"

Sergeant Gibson- "We got 'em, Bladge."

◂◈▸About the Authors◂◈▸

Ernest R. Twigg

Ernest R. Twigg was born into the Twigg family August 29th of 1976, the middle boy in a family of eight. In 1987 his sister Arlena passed away. During the autopsy, genetic testing uncovered the revelation that she had been switched at birth. He struggled in school and with his family throughout his teenage years. Dazed and confused, he talked to a Marine Recruiter. That talk influenced him to change his life.

Per Mr. Twigg's own assertion, the best decision he ever made came in 1996 when he joined the Marines Corps infantry. He earned his way to Sergeant before exiting service in 2000. He began an entry level position with the Brevard Group Treatment Home and worked his way up to third in the chain of command within one month. After the 9/11 tragedy, Sergeant Twigg switched to a paramilitary organization working in a maximum security state prison where he created the Brevard Correctional drill team and became part of the Florida Rapid Response Team dealing with riot control. In 2004 he went back into service to fight along his "brothers-in-arms" in Operation Iraqi Freedom as a Combined Anti-armor Team Section Leader and as a Scout Sniper Team Leader. He continues to lead Marines and is currently a drill instructor.

Robert S. Nahas

Robert S. Nahas is a professional book writer and president of Writer Services, LLC (www.WriterServices.net). He has thirty years of business experience in retail, manufacturing, and service industries.

Starting at the age of nine and running over a twelve-year span, Robert began to learn the business of business as well as customer and employee relations by working in grocery, restaurant, and other family-owned business-to-consumer establishments. At the age of 21, he put his experience and observation to the test by opening his first business on his own. During the eighteen-year existence of this successful sports and recreation retail store, he also established a manufacturing company. From this company, he is responsible for resurrecting a very famous fishing lure first invented in the 1940s called the Niantic Bay Spinner. This business-to-business experience further broadened his understandings of business itself, the people who interact within the business realm and the importance of good leadership for success.

Robert since has come to live out his true passion of writing books and offering an array of literary services through his company, WriterServices.net. He and his team of professionals deliver book writing, editing, proofreading, and every other possible necessity that aspiring authors might need for having a high-quality, successful book.

Robert S. Nahas has studied under some of the greatest educators and philosophers of our time, giving him a well-rounded perspective of not only business, but also human nature, human behavior, and human evaluation. Needless to say, his expertise in business and people skills is vast, uncommon, and invaluable.

Robert Nahas currently helps aspiring authors succeed, not only through well-written books, but also by engendering business savvy to his clients in order to succeed with the business side of books. He has led hundreds of people in the business world to great success. Eventually, he plans to retire and document all of his knowledge to share with the business world. In this book, *A Leader Provides*, he shares some of that information released nowhere else to date.

◁◇▷ Foreword ◁◇▷

*I*t is not essential to have been a Marine to be a business leader – but it certainly helps.

Business leadership takes many things: courage, skill, inventiveness, dignity, honor, and about fifteen or twenty other traits. This is something I know personally. Throughout my professional career, I have seen these skills in action at one point or another. Quite often, these abilities are used without plan or purpose, like driving a car aimlessly down a highway and hoping that you find the right exit.

Marines never do things that way. Even for the wet-behind-the-ears recruit stepping off the bus at boot camp, they have a plan and there is a purpose. Leadership plays a major role in that plan, in that purpose. The Marines didn't become one of the world's most elite military units by accident. They train and produce leaders, because leaders accomplish things...things that at an early perspective seem impossible. But leaders prove to produce results, and Marines are leaders by design.

The business world is exactly the same. Achievements don't occur in business by accident. They are created, brought about, made to happen. They are, in almost every case, the result of someone employing leadership qualities at a critical moment to bring about a desired result. "Good luck" in business is always the result of design...and design comes from leadership, from taking initiative and making things happen.

It always amazes me that more attention isn't placed on leadership in the business world. With scant observation one can easily predict the potential for success or inevitable failure. Time and again, the good leader wins the day. Groups lacking one go by the boards.

When the value of leadership is realized and good leaders are made, the secret to success in business and in life has been uncovered.

Marines produce leaders. Leaders are winners in business. With this book, you can learn how the Marines do what they do best – make the best leaders and get things done. And without a doubt, you can now apply those lessons to your career, and to your life.

— W.D. (Don) Mills, Jr.,
SIA Group President

⊰◇⊱ Chapter One ⊰◇⊱

Get On the Bus:
The Marine Corps' Tradition
of Leadership Excellence

◄◇► Chapter One ◄◇►

Get On the Bus:
The Marine Corps' Tradition
of Leadership Excellence

*T*he Marine Corps is actually older than the formation of the United States itself. Born in the heat of the American Revolution and forged in the fire of battle throughout that conflict and dozens of others over the years, the Marines are a unique military organization that has not only succeeded in countless formidable endeavors, but also stood the test of time. Equally at home on land or at sea, the Marines are the embodiment of honor, courage, and survival.

Testimony upon testimony exist about Marines getting the job done, triumphing over impossible odds. A major reason for their success is their understanding and utilization of leadership. It indeed does take a special type of person to make it as a Marine, yet their unparalleled and innumerable successes over the decades cannot be credited solely to the type of person involved, but also to the leadership imbued in those individuals.

Leadership is a virtue taught to Marine recruits the moment they stumble wide-eyed and anxious off the bus at boot camp. It never ends until a person leaves the Corps. During their time of serving, leadership is taught as intently and relentlessly as any other part of soldiering, as any other part of life. Leadership is as common and essential to a Marine as making one's bunk or taking apart and reassembling his or her weapon.

Even senior officers, men and women who have long since become accustomed to living the Marine life, receive leadership training throughout their careers. For the Marines long ago realized a simple truth: effective, intelligent leadership can overcome almost any obstacle and achieve almost any goal. Leadership is not a matter of lucky guesses or gut feelings or pie-in-the-sky hopes. It is a skill to be taught and learned and honed.

Switch out a uniform for a suite, replace the sword with an attaché case, and leadership is no different for the business world. But remarkably it is seldom thought of in the same way, as having such value.

Good leadership, whether for military or civilian needs, can rally a group of men and women, and whip them into a formidable force that can achieve nearly anything contrivable. All it takes is the right kind of leadership — proven leadership; leadership based on morals and optimum survival; superior leadership.

Though this might seem simple and mundane to some, this level of leadership is not so widespread as one might imagine. In fact, it is not even realized or understood. Because, if it were, it would be more widely used. Leadership is a business skill that is sadly lacking within many individuals and companies. It is given little attention, if any at all, once a person has been hired and has settled within the bosom of the company.

It is likely you have had a professional experience or two in which you ached for good leadership. The setting of the company that employed you was a besetting of one failure after another. There is nothing more dismaying than to watch something that we believe in or want to support or simply want to make a living from, that "could have been," "should have been," glorious and prosperous, go by the boards. If you happen to be so fortunate as to ever have been part of a company that exhibited enlightened and thoughtful leadership, you know then how remarkably beneficial the fruits of leadership can be.

The smartest approach to any endeavor is to obtain all the proven practical information that has been previously uncovered, and move forward applying those successful learnings. From that position, further experience and study can allow for the shortest runway to success. With the failure statistics of business being what they are, and the longtime, viable existence of the Marine Corps with their towering strengths being what it is... do you begin to see the benefit of learning leadership the Marine way and bringing those lessons to bear in the professional world?

More importantly, do you yourself want to be the best leader possible—the type of leader that achieves when others fail? The one that people look up to and want to emulate? The fact that you are reading this book would tacitly reveal that you do in fact want to be a good, even great, leader.

The fact that such an opportunity exists at all is quite incredible. In joining the Marine Corps, one can certainly become a great leader. But if one's life is not aligned for that, what can be done to learn the same proven leadership techniques and principles that the United States Marine Corps has used so successfully over the years? If another opportunity were to exist, it would have to contain the learnings, traditions, and concepts of the Corps. It would need to follow a similar path of teaching and it would require a strong understanding of the business world for it to work. The book you are holding is this very opportunity. It comprises the leadership learnings of a Marine and the experience and savvy of a business pro.

Know yourself and seek improvement. Those words are going to become quite familiar to you as you absorb the lessons from this book. For unlike other leadership books that simply list techniques and skills in rapid-fire order, with no time for reflection or thought, this book constantly asks you to take a review of yourself, be honest with yourself, and seek improvement where necessary. You are allowed to take time and reflect, for that is another skill that the Marine Corps teaches in tandem with leadership: Stop. Reflect. Improve yourself. This book will help you become a better business leader. And it will go even further by enabling you to become a better person.

Enjoy a Better Life

The list of famous Marines is long indeed and includes such luminaries as Senator John Glenn, baseball superstar Ted Williams, Fed Ex CEO Fred W. Smith, and newsman Dan Rather. What do all those gentlemen have in common? Leadership. They all seized the initiative at points in their life, ran with it, and became successful.

Business leadership takes courage. It also takes skill, ability, training, compassion, and a host of other qualities. Clearly it is not something you stumble into. Nor is it something best taught by reading theoretical suppositions or methods. True leadership is best taught by real-life experience – by others who have been through the trials and tribulations, and come out on top. For that's what makes this book special: it is filled throughout with leadership examples I have taken from my ongoing service with the Marines. These examples have come from real-life situations all the way from boot camp to Iraq. I have lived these examples – seen them make a difference in the everyday lives of men and women, sometimes operating among the most stressful and life-threatening conditions imaginable.

This book also contains the extensive business knowledge and expertise of my co-author, Robert S. Nahas. His real-life experience runs thirty years, officially, not counting an additional twelve years of working in retail and restaurant industries for his family, which began at the age of nine. In all, he has encountered people and the reality of the business world far beyond the norm.

5

No one can argue with the fact that the battlefield is a tough place in which to survive. And the business world is likely to be the second toughest place. In both scenarios there are sides taken and tough opponents wanting nothing more than total victory. So how does one win? What determines the winner? As can be witnessed from history, leaving things to chance or Divine Intervention are not practical, nor effective – especially when it is often all sides that are praying for Divine assistance. Though there is certainly nothing wrong with asking for strength from God, along with one's prayers must come leadership. And the most interesting thing about war and business is, the winners can be determined by which ones have the best leadership skills.

There's no place better to begin than my very own story, and how a life that was going nowhere fast was saved by Marine leadership:

In 1988, when my youngest sister, Arlena, died of heart failure on the operating table, chaos controlled my twelve-year-old mind. My behavior was already unacceptable in school and the grief only magnified my plummeting self-image. Fights with other children became more frequent than good grades, and my self-esteem began to drop like a thermometer in the Arctic Circle. I was uninspired, confused, and depressed; imprisoned by circumstances and careening out of control.

Just when things could not get any worse, genetic testing from the autopsy revealed that the girl I had grown up with and loved as my sister was not my biological sibling and had been switched at birth. My family was blitzed by a media frenzy, adding more instability and confusion to my already troubled teenage life. When the dust settled my family was in a state of shock, while I was growing up much too fast, hiding from the chaos of my uncontrolled emotions.

Desperate to fit in, I joined a gang and started a spree of violence and vandalism. At the time, it was an exercise of some control; no matter how poorly executed, it offered a sense of power and brotherhood, something I had longed for.

The problems inside of me manifested into problems at home, and instead of dealing with them, I ran away like a coward. With every violent outburst a piece of my happiness washed away as disappointment in myself grew. Preying on the weak did not display the honor I thought it would. My so-called "brothers" were complete hypocrites to the beliefs they professed, and I saw right through them.

I was heading on a crash course toward prison or death. I needed to change my route quickly. Then I had a life-changing experience—one that has brought me to my current station in life as a leader and motivator, and one that can help you also unlock the hidden leadership potential that exists inside all of us.

In August of 1995 a Marine recruiter met with me and insisted that I change my life. We sat down and he discussed words that my heart had longed to hear, such as honor, courage, and commitment. It was fascinating to find so many virtues being expounded that had eluded me for so long. All these characteristics I had sought for so long could be obtained by simply becoming a Marine.

Then he mentioned the word "integrity." I knew what it was but had never had the chance to live it. He offered me a way not only to explore other parts of the world, but also to visit places inside myself—all places where I had never ventured, but desperately wanted to traverse. It was my ticket to explore what I was made of. It was a fresh start to a stale and declining existence. This was my chance – possibly my only chance – to escape from a dead-end life, to prove to myself that I had the self-worth to be a leader.

On July 15, 1996 I decided to resurrect myself from a shallow life filled with failure, regret, and shame. I decided to really live again. "To be empowered and not imprisoned" – that was the Marine Corps way.

And it worked. I eventually found myself as a leader of men and women. I found that the self-worth and exceptional qualities I had always sought had been there all the time, buried deep inside of me.

The Marine Corps way worked for me. It made me a leader. And it can work for you. You have the power within yourself to be a leader. I hope, within these pages, to help you to unlock that potential.

Passing the Torch

Marines have a burning desire to share the gift that so many powerful leaders have passed from generation to generation. The Marine Corps has dramatically improved countless lives with the energizing and positive role that so many nameless leaders have played and still play today. It is an honor to be afforded this opportunity to represent one voice from the many who possess this knowledge. Most of the concepts described and elaborated on within this text come directly from Marine Corps orders. Motivation, dedication, spirit, discipline, honor, courage, and commitment: these ideas exist and are not forgotten inside of the hearts of those who believe and who believe in themselves.

Leadership takes belief. Molding a group of men and women into a cohesive unit capable of meeting their goal, whether it is field training or giving a sales presentation, takes a person who believes that he or she has the ability to perform the task. The next great leader could be you. Believe it.

Belief in self, country, and fellow men and women; the time to believe starts now.

Leadership feels good. Sharing your vision and inner belief creates a joy felt to the deepest parts of one's being. It empowers you to accomplish any task no matter what size. When you believe that your cause is just and you are benefiting everyone who surrounds you, the impact on your life is fascinating. Your confidence increases and your self-image improves. So many self-emplaced limitations start to simultaneously unlock and emerge for you.

Our potential as humans will never be completely understood. It does not have to be. Understanding our potential is secondary compared to operating without the limits we impose upon ourselves. Harnessing the potential of leadership creates a better version of us and therefore a better version of humanity.

How does a young person who lacks a direction in life and is in trouble with law enforcement go from a life of chaos to success? One of the most challenging times for humanity is the end of adolescence. Graduation creeps up and decisions about life dominate the thought process. It is an overwhelming time and the choices made come from adolescents not having the experience needed to understand the higher role they play in life. Think about someone you know who as a teenager struggled to find him- or herself and within months became something legendary, heroic or honorable. It happens more often than you might imagine.

Visualize the world's greatest military: The uniforms sharp and crisp, the drill steps performed in unison, so precise that they appear to be mechanical. Can you picture a clean-shaven and hard-chinned military person executing orders with superb bearing and demeanor? Now stop for a second and look at who you imagined. Was it a Marine? Their reputation for excellence has ensured them a place as an American Icon. They are the symbol of military precision.

This brilliant display of military transformation is so powerful that even a drug-torn teenager can become one of America's true heroes. In a matter of weeks people have beaten drug habits, poverty, criminal mentalities, gang affiliations, thoughts of worthlessness, and many negative or criminal issues. How many times have you heard the story about the youth in trouble with the law who joined the military and became a leader in society? How, as business leaders, can you harness that power? Leadership has an omnipotent, universal quality that can help every human regardless of color or creed.

How does the change in a troubled youth occur? Society has many assumptions on how the spiraling transformation takes place. This book challenges any skeptic who has had doubt about military leadership. The challenge is simple. Try to find the hate-filled senior yelling at the subordinate within these pages. You will strain your eyes trying, and they will be bloodshot and tired before you realize that this individual no longer exists.

Instead, what you will find in here is the positive effects that Marine leadership has on any human at any time. Negative understandings of how Marines lead are complete misrepresentations as to what truly occurs at any Marine base. The reality is that the Corps has invested millions of dollars in leadership education to change a lifetime of idiosyncrasies within a matter of months. This book highlights the core values instilled through hundreds of years of military experience and demonstrates how they can work for you. It is your guide for becoming a leader. Every person on every career path can prosper from these easy-to-apply fundamentals once you understand them and implement them into your daily routine.

Is there a way to tap into the phenomenal leadership that the Marine Corps has to offer? The answer is a big affirmative. The problem with most personal growth texts is that they try to sell you something new. But not this one. Marine Corps leadership is age-old leadership. Best of all, it is already in you. Your potential only needs to be discovered and unleashed.

Your search will start with the inner workings of you and as you apply these techniques, you will come to understand that you are not doing anything that is not a part of you already. You will be amazed at your ability to unlock your potential to accomplish any task.

Each individual who joins any branch of the armed services has different reasons to enlist. Millions of Americans have undergone the transformation and become millions of the world's finest citizens. They endured the challenges of boot camp so that the change would resonate in them forever. In three months, drill instructors transform civilian values into Marine values. By following their methods and techniques you too can become a molder of people and a role model extraordinaire.

You can become the same type of shining example in your place of business. You can become the person everyone wants to emulate; after all, everyone loves a winner. But also remember this: everyone respects a great leader.

The United States Marine Corps has been developing leaders since 1775. History reveals that Marines are natural leaders, either staying in service or transitioning into the civilian sector. In this book we investigate what drives a Marine to succeed, the power of his/her leadership traits and principles, and the importance of mission accomplishment. Most importantly, we examine how to put these traits to work for you.

The purpose of this book is to help any person increase their leadership skills in order to create a better lifestyle. If you want to increase your leadership skills, this is an excellent tool to do so. If you apply these simple, time-tested techniques, success will come from you leading the way. Leadership has no limits—you can apply this knowledge to business, academics, or any direction you are inspired to channel it. You can be in the military or be a civilian—these techniques will work for you. Leadership has no boundaries.

My life has been greatly enhanced by becoming a Marine. It thrills me to have been given an opportunity to lead men in combat and in garrison. Marine leadership created a successful civilian career that I only turned down to come back to where I belong. You may never have the need to become a Marine. Not everyone does. But I am certain that after reading this guide, you will have obtained the knowledge that will increase your leadership abilities, your inner motivation, and most importantly your overall happiness. Good luck and Godspeed. May your contributions not only help the world, but put it at your hands.

Your journey to a new life starts now. ◄ ◊ ►

◄◊► Chapter Two ◄◊►

The Art of Leadership:
What a Leader Needs to Know

‹◊› Chapter Two ‹◊›
The Art of Leadership:
What a Leader Needs to Know

*W*hat makes a good leader? What qualities must a leader exhibit that are looked up to, set a good example and generate respect and admiration? Would it surprise you to know that you probably possess many of these qualities? The secret is in unlocking them. If you can do that, you can become one of a select group of people – a leader of men and women. But how do you unlock their potential? To whom do you turn for answers and guidance? In the Marine Corps, recruits come in uncertain, unfocused, even confused. But they start living up to the challenges they face through the help of their drill instructor. They're shown how to unlock their potential in basic training. Often, there are no facilities or individuals to help us in the business world. This book will act as your personal basic training for leadership in your life. A leader's boot camp, you might call it!

Before any effective means of leading others can be effectively administered, it is necessary to understand what a leader is. In using some of the terms and descriptions that the Marine Corps uses to describe leadership qualities: motivation, understanding who and what you really are, team dynamics, brotherhood, situational awareness, and pride of belonging—we begin to see the make-up of an immense network of empowering values. These are the principles and virtues discussed in this chapter. They all work hand-in-hand, creating a better leader in you and ultimately, a better life for you and those you lead.

How is it possible to harness the amazing potential these qualities possess to make them work for you? We will explore just that subject. The Marine Corps has been finding these qualities in people for centuries, digging them up and bringing them to the surface, like a miner explores for and unearths gold. Once you discover how to find these qualities and understand how to utilize their full potential, you'll wonder how you ever got by without them before. But what needs to exist before anything else as a stabilizing foundation for successful leadership to develop is...

YOU HAVE TO KNOW YOURSELF FIRST AND FOREMOST.

Everybody should have at least one opportunity to meet someone great in their lifetime: someone so amazing that their inspiration can rarely be described and the legacy they leave affects generations to come. We can often find these individuals in educators. Many of us have stories about that special teacher who influenced so many kids. The lessons they taught are still used to this very day, some twenty, thirty, forty years later.

These types of individuals are extremely special. Notice the word "unique" was not used. This could imply that they cannot be matched or duplicated, they're one of a kind. But this is fallacy. Everyone possesses greatness. The only difference is that some have tapped into theirs all by themselves. And for this they are *very* special. Still, it is vitally important to realize that anyone with a good head on their shoulders, a compassion for their fellows, and a desire to help others succeed can be a significant positive influence—a great leader to others.

Fortunately, my co-writer and I have had the opportunity to meet endless numbers of outstanding leaders. I specifically had this honor and pleasure in the Marines. They all have had a positive effect on me at some point in my career and life. Out of all of the fish in the vast ocean of leadership, one sticks out in my mind like a Goliath. This is a leader who has a natural greatness shining from within and by example became a major influence on me and on my life. His name is Sergeant Robert "Sparky" Gibson II, a 26-year-old Ohio native who became Scout Sniper Platoon Chief Scout during my tour of duty as a Team Leader in combat from March of 2007 to September of 2007.

By this time I had the most Marine experience and had completed more deployments than anyone in the platoon. In addition, the Marine Corps had spent thousands of dollars on my leadership education and tactical proficiency. But seasoned as I was, Sparky maintained a higher status within the platoon for good reason. He was a natural-born leader of men and women.

Marine Snipers are the pinnacle of the Infantry. Over 70 percent of the Marines screened to join the platoon are dropped due to a failure to meet the demanding requirements. Then 30 percent of the rest drop out of the basic course once it starts. The physical and mental requirements are grueling, and include sleep and food deprivation. Not just anyone can be a sniper, let alone lead a sniper team.

Sparky was a great leader because of his dedication to his craft and his platoon members. He defined himself as a distinguished leader of the Infantry top elite. So why would he train us — and himself — to starve for days on end while getting minimal sleep and then run 10 miles in order to conduct an observation on a mock target located deep in the worst terrain possible? Why would someone who had nothing to prove constantly test their mental and physical limits in the name of training?

The answer to that question came to me as I watched this extraordinary leader control the morale and intensity of the platoon with his natural abilities. Sergeant Gibson possessed a leadership style that used a combination of philosophies. He knew he was great and didn't need anyone to tell him that, to reassure him. He achieved greatness by examining himself; he understood his strong points needed constant sharpening and his limitations would be lessened by constant improvement. He knew himself.

Sparky also displayed a fierce motivation that was infectious, while employing it on his team by understanding team dynamics. He instilled brotherhood and pride of belonging into all of his men and women—myself included—and he had an extreme amount of situational awareness and empathy. He knew each of his subordinates. So with this awesome role model I propose the questions: what is leadership, and what is a leader?

By structure and command line, a leader is someone located at the top. Leadership, by its very nature, is innately poised above all else. There can be sections within a whole organization, each with its own leader. Leadership goes hand-in-hand with other superior qualities, such as great pride, superior confidence, extraordinary greatness, and immense strength of will. It is impossible to effectively lead if one feels he or she lacks these heightened qualities. These attributes, that all leaders must have, need to be attained and maintained or else a poor example of "leadership" will be portrayed.

We humans have a tendency to view ourselves through the eyes of others. We base our personal perspective of ourselves upon the opinions of people who may be motivated by bad intent, jealousy, or any number of erroneous or ill-conceived notions. Because it is our human nature to have a disposition toward life as a game or competition, with a purpose to win and opponents and so forth, we can sometimes be perceived by others as a threat in their quest for whatever they may be striving toward. Seldom does this happen without lies, misconceptions or ill intent. This is a serious error on our part. How we may appear to others is not a clear reflection of ourselves, and it is detrimental to use such a gauge when determining our own self worth. If we accept the opinions of others as gospel, their "views" become limitations that we hold sacred, which greatly skews the perception of who and what we *really* are. For opinions to affect us, we would have to not know ourselves, or, more accurately, to not have confidence in our perception of ourselves.

This, then, is your first lesson, and something that the Marine Corps emphasizes from day one: Stop viewing yourself through the eyes of others. You, yourself, can conclude a much more accurate depiction of WHO and WHAT you really are. You are you, and no one has the right or qualifications to define yourself better than you – no one.

Then there are the distorted images of how we view ourselves personally. Often these images get manufactured during our developing years from things like when little Johnny was so proud of his painting, but his sister Katie laughed at it and said it was ugly; or when the beautiful girl who made his heart go pitter-patter shot him down cold when he asked her to dance. Then there were the times Johnny experienced failure head-on, the times he was oppressed, or countless other negative situations that caused him to "conclude" that he was not as great as he originally thought he was.

This "fall from greatness" is the beginning of the end of our personal confidence and happiness. For what are we without personal pride or self-esteem? We become someone who, to a greater or lesser degree, "believes" they lack worth and is incapable of accomplishing certain things. These feelings continue to accumulate as life goes on.

YOU ARE GREATNESS

The good thing about all of this is that the only thing holding a person down is the person himself or herself. In other words, we can become our own worst enemy by empowering our negative thoughts and inferior conclusions that we've drawn over the years. And the degree that a lack of greatness is considered real and valid determines the point at which one lowly exists.

It's amazing to think that we have to "agree" with negativity in order for it to have ANY effect on us. We have to say, "That's true. *You* are right about that." Why do we experience thousands of positive and great things and then when we receive a single negative comment from someone else, THAT is what we hold on to and let fester and believe to be true? The author is not here to resolve the minds of man, but to drive this point home: COME TO REALIZE WHO YOU *REALLY* ARE AND YOU WILL EMPOWER YOURSELF BEYOND BELIEF. It is certainly true that "You are what you think." This book will help you take a healthy look at yourself to see who's really standing in front of the mirror. Hopefully, one-by-one, any derogatory statements, degrading comments or inferior words that may be cluttering up the mirror will be wiped clean, and the greatness that you are will only remain visible to you and to others.

Everyone innately possesses the qualities of greatness,

but sometimes we can mask this greatness by how we view ourselves. That is the crippling factor for everyone. Thus the first step in the leadership process is for you to realize just who you really are.

Changing the Way You React to Negative External Influences

Begin this process of understanding yourself by ignoring what others think of you. Instead, create your own "personal value meter" and begin to draw a more accurate description of yourself. Divide your character traits into two general categories: Bad and Good. Are you considerate of other people? That goes under the "Good" column. Do you lose your temper easily? That gets listed on the "Bad" side. Once you have listed everything, read the unfavorable characteristics and acknowledge to yourself **without reservations** that these things are *not* who you are, but a manifestation of negative external influences.

As an aside, if you are having second thoughts, like "maybe I've overreacted at times and maybe I am actually a 'hothead'" or some other undesirable behavior, don't worry about it. These are still the effects of negative external influences, and this process is about changing how you react or respond to these influences. So you may not only need to work on how to deal with the negative things that people say about you, but also work on improving how you react or respond to the sometimes frustrating or irritating or agitating or wrong things that people do.

Now read the "Good" column and do the same thing, but this time acknowledge with **confidence and**

certainty that these favorable traits *are* who you are. And realize that the Good items are just a glimpse of the vast greatness that comprises you.

Believe in yourself. The Marine Corps teaches this basic but important lesson, and they turn troubled teens into leaders and doers on a daily basis. If these kids – some of whom come from broken homes and have no shortage of negative influences in their lives – can perform such a radical personality overhaul, you certainly can too.

No doubt there are many more great things about you that will become recognizable with time, dedication, and a steady striving for realizing that greatness. Helping you rediscover the merits and virtues inside you is part of what this book will help you achieve.

Here is another leadership question to consider: what makes a team follow a leader? The one-word answer to that is: Motivation. Motivation is a powerful force. It is what makes a group of Marines follow their leader into an unknown, uncertain fate. It applies the same in the business professional world.

Let's discuss how to make motivation work for you.

MOTIVATION

After many years in the Marines the question I have been asked the most is: "How do you maintain such a high level of motivation?" My answer is always the same. "I am fortunate to have discovered that I can achieve anything, therefore, *you* can achieve anything. I am no different in that regard".

We all have a mission in life, whether we realize it or not. My mission is to share with every Marine and civilian how understanding leadership can change your life. We all come from different backgrounds and have unique ideas. Having differences creates the variety in leadership styles any team needs to be successful. Yet there is one fundamental we all share and that is the need to be happy. Great leadership creates happiness for the leaders themselves and their subordinates. Accomplishment is the key factor in this.

It is a pleasurable experience to motivate others, plain and simple. It is what I do best and it is because of the Marine Corps that I have found the joy in this task. Having the ability to guide readers, business leaders, or Marines to a more productive and motivated state is a gift. Having inspiration and an inner fire to accomplish goals is nice, but what is awesome is watching people who felt the cold sweat of under-confidence and the stomach-wrenching vices of uncertainty push past those personal limits and achieve something better. Helping others achieve what they did not think possible is what life is all about.

I can remember a friend of mine who never left his couch, let alone his town or state. He joined the Marines because his parents told him that it would make him a man. Needless to say, he lacked motivation when he first came in. Not knowing what to expect and where his young life would end up, he was mired in a sea of self-doubt.

During boot camp he faced many exciting challenges he never expected. He completed obstacle courses, three-mile runs, and a demanding hand-to-hand martial arts program. Over the course of thirteen weeks the Marine Corps tested him mentally, physically, and emotionally. The whole time his confidence increased because his self-doubt was just an illusion. He started to learn that he could do these tasks and do them well.

We parted ways after boot camp but are still great friends and keep in touch to this day. He is now a motivated Gunnery Sergeant and is helping beginner Marines overcome those same doubts and fears that he once had. And he is now the man his parents knew he would become.

Please allow me to share another personal story with you on the value of motivation:

In January of 2006, while conducting a mobile security patrol in hostile territory, my squad was ambushed and one member was injured. The rest of us found ourselves trapped in the dilemma of facing hostile small arms fire while trying to conduct a medical evacuation for the injured Marine. The squad quickly and professionally swung into action. They neutralized the enemy, mitigated civilian damages, and got the injured Marine to safety and treatment.

The motivation displayed by every Marine in this real-life event is very easy to understand: preserve your own life and the lives of others as well. All this occurred naturally because the squad was motivated.

Hopefully you will not face anything as dire, but realize that the role of motivation is the same. It is the driving force that makes your team members swing into action with a specific goal in mind; be it saving a life or finalizing an important report.

What is motivation? Essentially, it is an inner desire that drives us to achieve a goal. The Encarta dictionary defines motivation as:

"1. The act of giving somebody a reason or incentive to do something.

"2. A feeling of enthusiasm, interest, or commitment that makes somebody want to do something, or something that causes such a feeling.

"3. A reason for doing something or behaving in a particular way."

As the first definition states, motivation means that *you are to imbue interest*, animation, enthusiasm, and/or excitement by reaching and affecting each of the members of your team. No matter what the goal—from making more money to saving lives—it is vitally necessary to know how to ignite desire in every member of a team.

The second definition shows *what it is that needs to be obtained* from within the team members. If there is no drive to accomplish a mission, it is impossible to achieve anything—at least anything of great value.

According to the third definition, *there must a purpose*. It can be about the goal involved, why the mission exists, why the necessary actions should take place, or why it is important that the outcome is brought about.

This brings up a very important point that must be understood. Someone on the team who does not want to achieve the desired goal(s) of the group is the same as someone not willing to pull the rope in a Tug of War game. Such a lack of contribution and support results in serious negative influences on the whole team, because the support of each member is expected and needed. It is a case of all but one pulling from the other end of the rope. This person is a liability to the entire team, as a whole and to each member individually. It is also important to know that no one likes to be alone in their efforts. People are starved for agreement, commonality, and camaraderie. Standing alone, they will diligently work at gaining unity with others. Therefore those who cannot be persuaded to strive for the common goal of the team must be removed or everyone will ultimately share the consequences of disparate goals within the group. Essentially, a Tug of War will ensue within the group itself.

So how do you inspire your people? How do you get them to *all* pull for the same goal? This is the first true test of a leader.

Remember that what might excite one person may turn another off. Because of this, you have to know what makes your people tick. Is it duty? Money? Is it simply the joy of attempting an almost impossible challenge? Whatever the things are that stir the souls of your team members, you must find ways to motivate each person. It boils down to knowing what will make each individual leap from their chair and be ready for action. (Under certain circumstances and last resorts, duress might be the best tool for motivation.) Motivation should be based on reason and survival of the group, as then it is not suppressive but for the greater good. Still, it is indisputable that a willing team member moving under his or her own willpower is the most loyal, trustworthy, and valuable of all.

There is an underlying factor – so significant and real that it could certainly be considered an axiom – that is known to the greatest of leaders: A SENSE OF URGENCY MUST EXIST IN ORDER TO MOTIVATE. Knowing this, it is possible for any leader to motivate ALL of his associates (except those with ill intent or another agenda).

Motivation can be spread from one individual to another. Often it begins with the leader, then is transferred to others through effective communication. The leader gives the reasons for doing something. In other words, he or she explains the purpose for their actions: "We're going there on foot so that the enemy doesn't hear us coming", "We're working all night because our largest client is arriving at eight o'clock in the morning and we're not ready for our presentation," and so forth. Whatever the leader has them do, it is always for a desirable outcome. Here are some ways to spark the inner fire of motivation that will work if you understand and implement them on a consistent basis:

SET GOALS

Without predetermined direction and a point to reach, motivation is uncontrolled and wasted effort. The energy and creativity that spawns from motivation can be harnessed and used most effectively when implemented into the overall plan for attaining your goal. It makes no difference who you are motivating: your team, other leaders, or yourself. You need to focus on a specific result.

ENCOURAGE YOUR TEAM

Complimenting someone else's work shows your attention to their abilities and generates vitality. Encouragement acknowledges the progress your subordinates have made, and as a corollary, what appeared to be a formidable task becomes smaller because team members see the fruits of their labor. Remind yourself to encourage anyone at any time when it is deserved. Too often, the head of a group or team only corrects and reprimands, which creates an imbalance and excess of negativity. The process of encouragement, as simple as it is, can produce the most amazing response from your team and the rewards are boundless.

PROVIDE INCENTIVES

People love rewards and will work hard for them. It is a true yin and yang of productive environments. Thinking that a paycheck is all that is needed for hard work falls far short of understanding what a strong, bonded, workable relationship needs in order to exist between employer and employee, leader and team. After a few weeks or months of employment, a paycheck is to be expected. If you want to motivate, then it becomes necessary to go above and beyond. Think outside the cashbox.

Understand that people are different, so your incentives will differ from one person to another. The easiest way to figure out what it is that will make people put more "oomph" into their mission or activity is to simply ask. Survey the group and ask what they would want if this or that goal were to be achieved. This goal would need to be a difficult target that could realistically be attained if they put their minds to it. The target must be clearly defined, including the completion date or time, as well as all other relevant specifics. All should be understood by the people who will be making the attempt. The reward could be for the individual who did the task best or it can be for the entire group. The size of the target needs to match the size of the reward. In other words, the reward needs to suit the achievement. You would not offer a new company car to someone for making the most sales calls to customers. Nor would you give a piece of cake for a million-dollar sale for a small company that normally does 500K annually.

If the activity is long-term, the smart leader starts out with a small incentive and works his or her way up from there. You'd be surprised at what the smallest of rewards can do for morale. A free trip to the movies, an extra half-hour off for lunch, or a week/month/year in the "Top Performer" parking space located right outside the front door of the building, or something similar can be great incentives. Then, as the activity grows, so too could the rewards. What would determine if it were necessary to continue incentives is whether people still responded favorably to them. Greater incentives could include a weekend trip to Las Vegas, a ticket on one of those local Cruises to Nowhere, a fancy "leased" car for three, six, or twelve months, dinner for two at a nice restaurant...the possibilities are endless. But again, the incentives that are going to create the most excitement are those stated by the players themselves that THEY want as a reward. If things become stale after awhile and no one comes up with another idea, you can offer three of four possibilities of your own for them to vote on.

The magic behind this is that a challenge is presented with a reward at the end of it – the proverbial carrot on the end of a stick. This is not to imply that the subordinates are "suckers." That would be a degrading and ignorant view of the people who make things happen for you. Always remember that those who have a high level of willingness to forward the overall goal are your most valuable, precious, priceless assets – without exception!

Some people will view the challenge that you present as a game, something fun and exciting. To others it will be a mountain to climb, something adventurous to overcome. In any case, creating incentives raises the productivity rate by raising spirits, raising the stakes. Incentives can make a game or challenge out of something that could just as easily be viewed as drudgery, formidable, or boring. Implement incentives on a regular basis and watch your subordinates' motivations, and productivity, soar.

TEAM DYNAMICS

The term "team dynamics" is essentially defined as

'the unseen forces that exist within a group of people.' They are the result of the overall actions and motives of a group of people. Every interaction with another human is a form of team dynamics. It is worth mentioning, in order to bring attention to it, that there can be good and bad dynamics within a team. A team with poor or weak team dynamics will eventually fail, or never get off the ground in achieving anything worthwhile. A team with bad or destructive dynamics within it will disband or destroy itself in time. So it is important to monitor the overall feel or essence of your team and strive to only possess team dynamics that will allow for the achievement of the intended goal. Having the ability to motivate and mold people to work together is an awesome tool.

I have had the chance to lead hundreds of Marines in a variety of infantry-related fields. It is extremely difficult to keep tabs on all of them, but for the most part we keep in contact. Their personalities vary from one extreme to another. One Marine, I will call him Lance Corporal Johnson, had very complex social problems because of his history. He was home-schooled and, while he may have received a good education, his adolescent years were not provided with adequate social development. He was a good kid with a solid foundation of values and traits. However, social interaction was an area he needed to work on.

When Lance Corporal Johnson first came to the unit, he was too shy to speak with authority and confidence. He mumbled when he talked so that his words could not be understood. He had a way of interacting that made an easy exchange of ideas into a long, drawn-out affair. His shyness was so severe that he tried to avoid most team activities. With an inability to communicate, his dropping out of school for a more secluded environment at home had reinforced his shy personality and introspective attitude. As a leader, the greatest problem with avoiding your team is that it doesn't demonstrate confidence and imbue trust in your team members.

But in the Marines no one can drop out when they have issues. Each must face them. Placing Lance Corporal Johnson into a team gave him the chance to build his confidence and social skills. Forced outside of his comfort zone, he worked hard on being more assertive and breaking the confinements of his shy nature. He was assigned to give classes on public speaking and leadership in order to increase his social abilities.

It was the team that increased his standard. He worked hard to meet the expectations that were placed on him through his comrades. In turn, a solid team was built upon a firm foundation of trust. He learned the immeasurable value of what a team is, he absorbed the essence of team dynamics – how to survive as a team – and he implemented what he had learned among all of the members of the teams that he led.

As the years went by, this shy boy developed into an assertive leader. That timid façade was covering up the values that made him admirable, but in time he confidently developed the ability to articulate those virtues. To this day he is expressive and confident while running his own small business, and he uses the leadership skills learned in the Marines; the same skills you are coming to know.

Leaders understand that harnessing competitive initiative will develop motivation in subordinates. Having a sense of selfless camaraderie is important to the competitive, changing world because, for one thing, the individual does not want to let his team members down. Why did the Spartans at Thermopylae sacrifice themselves? The answer is because they did not want to let others down. Imagine what possibilities await a team whose members possess a sense of heroism, the willingness to make sacrifices all for the glory of success and the attainment of the overall desired goal. This would be an unstoppable team. Instill a sense of unwavering selflessness in your team members and you will witness amazing heroism and courage from people who may never have known they possessed such admirable qualities. One way of instilling this is through example.

The leader demonstrates from the front and gets beside his subordinates. He or she is not above them in greatness, except perhaps by being imbued as a greater leader *because* of one's team members. The leader is a *member* of the team and not an outsider directing the herd. Creating team initiatives and team-building experiences is a fundamental goal of the Marine Corps. The strength of a unit is not because of a single person, but the complete chain. We all have heard that the group is only as strong as its weakest link. This can be easily proven true. But what is quite amazing is the realization of just how strong a chain gets when it is linked to itself, full circle.

When opposing forces are pulled on such a chain, it can be considered at least twice as strong due to its doubling up. But in real life among humans, possessing positive team dynamics and with the fortitude of knowing that a team also includes its leader, such a group could be analogized as having its links melded together in equilibrium and possessing a strength that is at least squared. This, in the author's view, is a conservative assessment of the potential power of a team. As some leaders in the business world have mistakenly excluded their connection with their teams, this metaphor of the chain appropriately describes the strength of the team with ALL of its members realizing that they are actually members, especially its leader.

A team should be given a common purpose or goal. These goals are objectives and are passed on through the chain of command. The ultimate goal of a team might be one that is very large. In such a case, short-term goals can be set, which lead the group toward the larger goal. In any case, start with attainable goals, and watch as the unit begins to act as a team and win as a team. With each accomplishment, aside from the trust that builds, you will find that each member learns one another's strengths and weakness, and the strong will pick up the slack for or carry the weak.

After the team has had time to adjust to each other and they are able to carry out a few tasks, they are ready for greater tasks. With a reward envisioned, the team will dedicate themselves to the cause of victory for the teammate to the left and the right. However, teamwork and competitive nature alone do not solely make up the drive to succeed. Many characteristics of a person make him or her an important player for each task assigned. Using a team member within his or her capabilities is the key. A successful leader in the Marines does not use a Marine who did poorly on his physical fitness test to perform the physical portion of a challenge. Instead he finds the strength of that individual and finds him/her a more suitable challenge.

Similarly, a business leader does not place someone who is bad at math in charge of tallying up final sales figures. A good leader understands the strengths and weaknesses of his or her team members, and places people in positions in which they can excel and the team as a whole can utilize their strengths.

Let's look at what we have discussed thus far:

What can you do for your employees right now that will start them acting as part of a team? What project can you start to get team dynamics working? Take a pen and outline the ideas you have to increase teamwork. Once you test and review these ideas and feel comfortable that they work, turn them into policy to be followed from there on out.

Once the projects are started and you have your groups broken down, give them incentives. Remember that simple, individual recognition can mean more than a raise. Use teamwork as a tool to critique and discover any friction amongst team members. Identify strengths and weaknesses among your group members and allow the team the freedom to place individuals where they are best suited. Make sure you appoint a speaker for the team. This needs to be someone who stands out and can give direction with confidence and ease. Your direct subordinates should then follow the lead of the person who best meets that position. This individual will assume the role of Group Leader.

Once the team members have worked together and smoothed out the kinks, add competition between them. Maybe you could add excitement by giving awards for the team that accomplishes the most in the time period directed, or the one that achieves a certain sales figure. The possibilities are endless. Provide incentive for the whole team and demonstrate how it pays to be a winner. You will discover that the overall work environment will increase: productivity will be up and morale will be higher. When a team works for a greater goal the will to succeed starts to manifest itself in the efforts of your team members. Everyone is a winner—they just have to believe it themselves. You must make them believe it. Now you can see why it is important that you believe in your own innate abilities. If you do not believe that you're a winner, how can you impart this feeling to others?

BROTHERHOOD

What are the rewards for being inspired? Does the leader have to be the only one to share his or her motivation and desire to create a better workplace? Think for a moment about the people we are most loyal to in the world—our very own families. We love them for all they do right and despite all they do wrong. We help them, and the favors are returned tenfold.

Many people confuse team dynamics with creating a family environment, i.e., brotherhood. Team dynamics is the ability to group people together and use them effectively. They are dependent upon each other to get the job done. Brotherhood is a selfless virtue that places emphasis on the members you serve much like a family environment. We have all heard the cliché "a band of brothers." Those words are so accurate that Marines have laid down their lives so that others can carry on. The love for the other creates a passion to not let anyone down. In business, it creates an environment in which teammates want to assist each other to the best of their abilities.

The Marine Corps has one of the greatest networking systems in the world. Imagine thousands of people who consider you a "brother" and are willing to help you with what you are looking for. One and all follow a few basic principles: Take care of your own and show people that they mean more to you than just numbers; assist a comrade to the best of your ability; it never hurts to be too helpful; and provide all of the details and go above and beyond the call of duty for each other. These principles, taken together, develop a brotherhood. It does not come quickly or easily—it takes time and trust. You, as a leader of professionals, should implement a similar set of guidelines to follow. What has worked so well for the Marine Corps can work just as well for you in the business world.

PRIDE OF BELONGING

Having pride of belonging to a certain group is an important team concept, and something that the Marine Corps has successfully instilled in leaders for decades. Have you ever met a Marine who was not proud he or she was a Marine? They embody the pride of belonging.

As a leader, ask yourself if you have instilled the pride of belonging in your team members. It's easy to do: Have you taken them out to lunch and paid for it? Have you given credit where credit is due? Have you shown appreciation for their hard work? Don't ever take over on a responsibility that you have assigned to another, unless there is impending danger or ruin that this individual is incapable of overcoming. It is vitally important to allow your team members to experience pride through a job well done. This is one of the greater joys of life. Let them know, whatever they do, that each individual and the team as a whole has done, or is doing, very well. Don't just provide lip service, but demonstrate how proud you are of the entire team from top to bottom.

A leader needs to have patience. If someone is talking trash behind your back let them expose themselves for who and what they are to the team. Members of the Corps are told quite often that there are no bad Marines, just bad leaders. With enough patience, most everyone comes around to accepting the fact that they are the best at what they do. Embrace that concept and put it to work for you.

Every time you win a competition or a challenge,

emphasize that it was not you but "the team" that won it. Allow them to internalize how well their efforts paid off. Give credit where credit is most certainly due.

Point out the differences between your team and others. Hold them to a higher standard and show them how they differ from others because of that standard. Maybe your team is more cost efficient and has higher productivity than the other. This needs to be brought to your team members' attention in order to give them a sense of pride. Hold them to the unit's standard and allow them to be proud of where they come from.

KNOW YOUR PEOPLE

There is a problem often encountered in life: some people act like they know their job, but actually do not. They talk a good game, but when it comes time to put in the work they fall short. We all know the type. Even the Marines have them. The problem is universal. This is one reason why it's so important to know your job. What responsibility, as leaders, do we have to increase the drive to succeed in any team member? How can we make individuals do more for less? The answer is by knowing them.

Take a sincere interest in your people. Understand and implement their strengths and seek to minimize their weaknesses. This is an exciting principle that increases morale, productivity, and loyalty for the employer and employee. One increases morale simply by allowing others to work and take pride in their jobs. Tell them what to do and then let them get the job done. They will burn the midnight oil getting to complete the action or achieve the status, just for the freedom alone that you've granted them. And if there's loyalty present, they'll practically jump through fiery hoops for you. How is loyalty built? When you are sincerely concerned for a team member's safety and well-being, family life, or personal relationships, that person is more apt to demonstrate loyalty to you. Loyalty is something of depth, something that a simple paycheck will not by itself breed. It is the same whether practiced in the Corps or in business: knowing your Marines or knowing your employees, and looking after their welfare will increase their work output exponentially. In business, acting with reserve and investing some concern for the employees demonstrates your loyalty.

If someone is doing poorly at a task that they normally excel in, for example, it would be wise and advantageous to ask if everything was all right and whether they would like to talk about whatever is on their mind. All too often, employers are insensitive to the personal issues of employees. "Work and home are two separate matters and should be left that way." But realize that the spirits and emotional state of one of the members of a team affects all of its members' performances. Taking time to allow a worker to vent can be beneficial. And it's an opportunity for instilling loyalty and creating a gung-ho attitude by showing just how important and valuable he or she is to you and the team. You'll find that they'll push past the block and resume, if not exceed, their level of proficiency.

How many bosses have you had that didn't accept

feedback from their employees? It creates a rift of resentment between the two sides. We all know the cold and calculating boss who makes statements like: "This is your job. If you don't like it find another one." How does this increase any worker's output? Threats and negativity only create a hostile work environment, especially when the workers deserve praise. Imagine how good it would make others feel if once in a while someone were to stop by and ask how things were and if they needed anything.

This applies to all levels of management, from the lowest to the highest. It does not matter if you have one employee or 100. You should check on the happiness and morale of your employees. Gauge them and then decide whether intervention is needed. This is your responsibility as a leader. How are your team members doing today? Be sincere and demand an honest answer, not a typical response, like "Yes boss, everything is great."

When you demonstrate concern, the workplace begins to adapt to your philosophy. The people who run your company start to check up on each other, and the baselines are set. Take a few minutes out of your busy day to get to know the investments you have working for you. Let them know they make a difference.

Too many managers see positive reinforcement as a potential trap that will only aid the justification for pay raises. Think about the military when you break down the pay scale. Basic recruits get paid approximately $2.60 per hour, based on the basic pay chart and hours worked in boot camp.[1] Think about how hard they work for that $2.60. They work hard for their leaders – not for money. Such worries from business managers of "swelling heads" and "pay increases" creates the inevitable environment deprived of all the favorable traits, including loyalty, high productivity and pride. The sad part is, if such a manager were to ever have an environment possessing such admirable traits, there would in fact be no need to worry about pay raises, as there would be sufficient money on hand, and there would be great expansion, and all of the other ideal upshots. This unacceptable and oppressive "leader" has no place in the business world or anyplace for that matter, and certainly has no business leading at all. Such individuals only lead their subordinates to places like dead ends, down wrong roads, and off of cliffs. If you have found yourself in such a mindset from time-to-time, don't fret just yet. Realize that it is likely that you have listened to the perspective of someone else whom you may have considered successful. But such people are not happy individuals, and most don't stay "successful" for very long. Just realize that this means of "good business sense" is nothing but a part of bad business practices. Reward those who deserve reward, praise those who deserve praise. You'll sleep better and your own rewards will be greater.

Know yourself and seek self-improvement. Do you check on the welfare of your employees? Are you aware of the morale at your company? Are you viewed as an

---

[1]http://www.dfas.mil/militarypay/militarypaytables/2008MilitaryPayCharts35.pdf

outsider to your people or a part of the team? Are you considered a good leader by your subordinates? Understanding yourself is the key to understanding other employees.

Establish a comment box so you can feel the pulse of your workers. Allow people to voice things that are taking place without fear of being black-balled or labeled as a whistle blower. Even when serious violations occur most employees do not want to report them if they can't be anonymous.

When a team feels connected to their leader, the drive to succeed is manifested and nothing can stand in their way. The team has only the limits set by the commander.

You've heard the saying, "You can please some of the people some of the time, but you can never please all of them all of the time." Don't expect something more than this. That would be expecting the impossible, an assured lost cause. If you operate with integrity and do your best for the company and your team, you may still have the occasional stubborn individual who does not want to respond to your direction. Have the courage to document this behavior and then cut your losses after you try to fix the problem. Low morale is a virus that spreads, zapping the life out of any cause. If the problem is irreparable, then as a leader it is your responsibility to the company and the team to identify it, resolve it, or remove it from the environment. For that you need situational awareness.

SITUATIONAL AWARENESS

Situational awareness is a capability that, when developed, increases the quality of your work. Nothing can compare to actively paying attention to what is taking place. Your projects will be streamlined if you oversee the direction of productivity and troubleshoot problems that may arise. If you display situational awareness and then ask your teammates for their understanding of the situation, it increases their attentiveness. Remember that two eyes are better than one. Together, your working minds oversee the direction of the product and make cost-effective decisions before problems arise.

Being part of a team makes it easy to increase situational awareness. Sometimes it is as simple as telling the team members you need them to turn on their thinking caps for the upcoming task. Incorporate them into your planning process and then supervise. Do not blindly trust them to do it all and do it right, because humans love to take the path of least resistance. Instead, supervise them and interact. That's what you're there for, and they need you for this purpose. Be aware of each person's impact. Ensure that they are meeting the necessary benchmarks. Reward the deserving and reprimand those who fail to pull their weight. Over time you will learn who your "go-to" employees are. These are the pillars of the company or group, the people you can count on for the most complex tasks or when the chips are down. They are your money-makers, and the folks you should invest the most effort in rewarding.

In the Marine Corps situational awareness is vital. Lives could be lost if a leader is not constantly aware of the situation. Even in basic training, people can be seriously injured if a leader misjudges the situation. That's why a leader in the Corps always has to be on their toes...or, in other words, demonstrate situational awareness.

A FINAL WORD

The human drive to succeed is exemplified by the Marine Corps and their ability to develop leaders. There are countless examples in Marine Corps history that show that leaders can be made. By implementing some of the steps and methods we have covered in this chapter, you will start to develop as a leader or improve from the one you are no matter what environment you may have to endure. From a combat field to a desk, leadership is necessary to maximize favorable results and increase work performance.

Your journey to leadership will take you and your teammates to unimaginable heights. You will accomplish what appears at first to be impossible and raise the standard of excellence as long as you allow yourself to grow. Understand that whatever circumstances you are in at this very moment, you can achieve more. ◄◊►

‹◊› Chapter Three ‹◊›

How the Core Values of the Marines Turn People Into Leaders, and What Those Values Are

◁◇▷ Chapter Three ◁◇▷

How the Core Values of the Marines Turn People Into Leaders, and What Those Values Are

*N*o one wants to be the weak link. Each team member struggles to become better, while you as the leader help and guide them. But it is possible to become too engrossed with your subordinates to realize where you, as the leader, stand. Without knowing how we look from the perspective of our employees, it is quite possible that we ourselves are the weakest link! This disconcerting surprise can be remedied through the observation of certain things. Do not confuse employee observation and constructive criticism as a personal attack. Try to avoid taking any criticism personally.

Consider good leaders for a moment – people in any capacity, such as a sports coach who leads his team to win the pennant, an employer who has hundreds of loyal employees who are happy to come to work, or a government official who leads a sector of state or country.

What virtues do they have? Why do people look up to them? How are they able to instill such confidence and dedication in others to follow them?

One reason these leaders succeed at what they do is because people seek to hold a common belief among one another. When people believe in a cause in which they are allowed to help and they can trust in the person they follow, there exists great benefit for all concerned; this not only includes the immediate group, but others outside who may have a need or interest in what "the cause" produces.

Something as seemingly simple as a baseball team can produce escape from the hustle-bustle of life for a few hours for many people. A group working to help stop some injustice might help millions of people from their efforts. A business that produces a product of necessity makes a difference to many thousands of people.

Any group possessing a common belief is prime for nurturing very effective teams. Add to that, if you can, a situation where no one is there to work solely "for the money," and you've got a rare and unstoppable recipe for immense success. In most cases, employers and others who lead use money as the "priority" in building their groups. Granted, it is a needed element, without question, but money by itself has never produced the greatest groups. That's because it is impossible without more favorable motivations, such as "duty," believing in a cause and having trust in one's leader.

Would you believe in a fraud or someone who stole credit for something that you had worked hard on? How about a person who spoke one way behind someone's back and another way in front of them? The answer is obviously no. You may even know someone like this yourself. If you do then you understand that believing in your leader is one of the hardest things for a team member to do. This belief does not happen overnight. Rather, belief in a leader comes from trust and reputation – the feeling that you can follow this person anywhere, and you will not be betrayed.

Ask yourself what virtues you identify with when you believe in and put your faith in a person. Almost certainly all of the virtues mentioned so far in this book. It then becomes obvious that if these virtues were to be utilized correctly by yourself, the result in the workforce or on any team would be very positive, and your relationship with your employees or team members would be rock-solid.

Members of the Marine Corps are taught to trust their leaders, with the result that they will follow them anywhere, even into the heat of battle with bullets whizzing all around them and the rank odor of death heavy in the air. Why will these men and women unquestioningly follow their leaders into potentially deadly situations? It is because they believe in them – it's nothing more complicated than that. A simple act of faith can work wonders for a leader, either on the battlefield or in the boardroom.

What are the values that the Marine Corps teaches to inspire such loyalty and devotion to their leaders? They are simple but powerful: honor, courage, and commitment. When taken together these values constitute an amazing block of trust, faith, and belief that any leader wants and needs to possess.

Let's examine these values in detail:

HONOR

In today's society it sometimes seems as if honor has almost become a forgotten word. Many teenagers would likely not be able to give a correct definition of it. Even a look into modern dictionaries reveals that a clear, somewhat indecisive understanding of it. Honor has become a concept that is somewhat abstruse. Yet, it is certain that we all would hope and expect to be treated honorably. Perhaps if more teenagers, and even some adults, knew what it meant, more would live by its principles.

Dictionaries define honor as having "high regard" or "respect." Though these qualities are certainly aspects of honor, they fail to fully explain its unique and complex existence. In recent times there have been individuals who try to associate honor with military chivalry. This devalues the importance of honor in society. And yet, when we honor something, such as a cause or belief, we authenticate our lives. We live by who and what we truly are and what we strive to be. Therefore, it is important, if not imperative, that the concept of honor be better understood.

Honor takes on many forms of value and worth. Indeed, it is a landscape on which the Marine Corps has successfully trodden for many years, and should be walked on by you in your role as leader; it must be if you wish to be the best of leaders. The values of "respect" and "holding with high regard" encompass a lot of moral territory, but there is more to it. Other virtues associated with honor are "paying homage" and "demonstrating loyalty to those you respect," and "glorifying and rewarding the deserving."

My co-author, Robert, probably has the most succinct way to explain honor: The upholding of the ideal qualities of a social area, which would then deserve respect and a sense of worthiness. Honor is a two-way street; one can honor others and one can be honored. In both cases, it is something to be earned, something deserving by one's combined actions of the *highest caliber*. This above definition explains honor for any walk of life, whether it be for self, a personal relationship, a career, groups or any other areas of social intercourse.

In the business world, "the earning side" of honor might be defined as having the qualities of "trust" (keeping one's word) and "pride" (in one's work). It might include "quality" (of one's products or service) too. Certainly, someone who was trustworthy, produced quality products and took pride in their everyday affairs would deserve honor from others. And there surely can be more qualities, but none of which would include the sometimes used excuse for unethical action – 'all being fair in love, war, and business.' So understand that being ruthless, for example, though it might make someone wealthy in finance, there is no honor in cut-throat activities or dog-eat-dog tactics. And such individuals lack true wealth—that of having worth to their contemporaries, the people in his/her life. Sure, one might have a lot of money, but what good is it if he has no friends, but only enemies, those who fear him and those who want to get even? Honor is at the extreme opposite end of this scale of doingness.

In the educational realm, say, as a teacher, Dean, Principle, Guidance Counselor, Truant Officer, or even someone who answers the telephones, the qualities honor might be "honesty, truthfulness and caring." Again, though there could be more, these would be extremely valuable qualities, for the youth of our nation, and the world for that matter, deserve to be educated with true information about things. And those who run the show should be honest with them and caring about their progress and growth.

In the military, honor might be possessing and displaying true "courage, trust, and dependability." Courage would be a necessary and valued quality of the battlefield for self and one's team mates. And showing others, by your actions, that they can trust and depend on you...well that's allowing others (and yourself) to honor you. And as your teammates conduct the same qualities, they too deserve your honor of them. This is the two-way flow of honor.

As honor is certainly paying respect and support and even reverence to another or others (this is the more common understanding), there is the other side of the coin of "being" a certain way: upholding the finest qualities most valued in a specific area of life. The reason why this concept it being worked on so diligently here is because "honor" can be glibly applied. Being nice, following orders "because one has to," saying "good morning" because it's the socially polite thing to do, does not cut it. It is worth restating here that honor is has to do with the highest of qualities. And the way that we best pay homage others is to uphold those qualities relentlessly, sincerely, and continuously.

A great importance in the interaction of two or more people – or even with yourself, alone – is how we act, the way we conduct ourselves. To earn honor from others and to give honor to those who have earned it is to have a unique and solid bond of the highest kind.

Marines narrow the focus of honor from a broad territory to a refined area of critical interest by following four important personal principles that cater to the individual:

1. Honor yourself by staying true to your words.

2. Honor your religious convictions, what-ever they may be.

3. Honor your family because we wear our family name on our chest.

4. Honor your country, for this land is what we fight for.

We do the right things, we exude the best qualities through our actions, in order to continue the existence of something worth upholding.

These Marine values mean that "I will not bring shame upon myself, God, family, or country." Much like the Samurai warriors of Japan who honored the warrior code known as the Bushido, the Marines honor a very personal philosophy known as Marine Corps values. (However, Marines do not limit themselves to just this set of moral principles but practice others as well, which is why the Corps produces such exceptional leaders.)

Do your employees feel from the inside of their hearts that they have the honor and distinction to work as your team? These are the feelings that you want to create among them. Creating honor is a process of honoring traditions, customs, loyalty to the cause, the feeling of contribution, upholding the highest standards, and the pride of belonging.

Allow yourself to feel how honored you are to be surrounded by professionals. Embrace the true people who support you and let them know they are special and elite. Actions speak louder than words, so show them how important they are to the overall team effort. Above all, keep these attitudes consistent. Your team members will quickly lose their belief in you if your attitudes toward them change like the wind or you become whimsical and unpredictable.

Discuss differences and try to bring solutions to the table. Show respect to the members of your team who pay homage to you. Do not say things merely to curry favor, and do not reward those who are not loyal to you. The people you lead are watching and they want to believe in someone who will fight for them. That someone must be you. You are their leader. Once they observe your honor they will emulate it.

Honor is the hallmark of a Marine. Honor is the bedrock upon which a successful leader builds his or her team and meets all challenges. Let honor be your bedrock in the business world as well.

COURAGE

Courage is the capacity to meet danger or difficulty with firmness. There are two types of courage: Moral and physical. Marines will tell you that physical courage, such as getting shot at and continuing onward, is much easier than telling a friend he has a drinking problem. Moral courage requires a special individual; it is one thing that separates the great leader from the would-be great leader. Moral courage is what we will discuss next. It is easy to understand but difficult to execute.

What does moral courage mean? It means having the intestinal fortitude to make corrections and do the right thing, even when no one is watching. It means to speak with firmness and fairness, and resist the temptation to sugar-coat things to your favor. A leader with moral courage provides on-the-spot corrections, and gives guidance when needed – not just mindless criticism when things fail to go a certain way. Moral courage **does not mean** taking over a project as your own and micro-managing it. You must find the moral courage to lead by example – a trait that is harder than it looks. Yet a true leader, one who respects and is respected by his/her team, exhibits moral courage. As a result, the team responds and soon acts the same way. Hold yourself to the standard that you expect from your employees, and watch them follow your example.

The Marine Corps has been watching this phenomenon occur for years. Members of a squad or company may have little or no personal interest in trying to achieve a certain goal. Yet the leader acts with such moral courage and sets such an indelible example that the members feel driven, if not guilty, to give 110 percent for him or her. They are literally inspired by the example set by their leader.

A group that previously had no interest in the goal becomes willing to do whatever it takes to achieve it when their leader's moral courage is such that they would be ashamed to let him or her down.

Finding the integrity to do what's right even if it is against the norm takes a large amount of moral courage. For example, defending a co-worker from peer pressure shows your inner strength to other members of your team. Still, not every exhibition of moral courage should be for your team members' appreciation. You should find the courage in yourself to do the right thing, because it's the right thing to do. Many problems occur because employees don't have the courage to work through difficult situations. As their leader, you must instill that courage in them. You can do this by example: courage will encourage.

Sometimes displaying moral courage gets in the way of your career, and you have a critical decision to make. This is a time when you can find out whether or not you have moral courage. If a supervisor did something wrong and you had the moral courage to identify it, you would be soothed by the fact that you did the right thing. You would have exhibited moral courage.

Our motives and actions all tie in to courage. If you were to blow the whistle on someone just because you didn't like him, such motives are simply destructive and not based on anything admirable. However, if you reported something because the violation or wrong-doing may have hurt someone else, then you did the correct thing. Motives of integrity will set one's mind at ease.

Do your teammates work for you because they need a job? This mentality produces limits and discourages the will to work hard. If someone is inspired and loves what they do, the boundaries of the endeavor spread outward and limits become limitless.

You, as their leader, need to provide the needed inspiration, just as leaders in the Marines provide inspiration to their team. Find the courage to believe in yourself. Believe in your cause or what you work for. Once you do that, you can share this point of view with your teammates. Have the courage to profess your vision with integrity and without self-prejudice. Inspire people with your honest fascination and determination; allow your personal inspiration to act as a healing flame, disintegrating negative thoughts that could hold them back, and allowing the growth of belief that will take them to new heights. Trusting in yourself takes courage. Putting trust in others also takes courage. Growth becomes natural when you have the courage to remove limits.

Do you know what limits are? They are not walls and boundaries and solid objects. A thirty-foot wall is no limit to a man who knows he can scale it in a matter of seconds. Limits are the critical thoughts that prevent one from being able to accomplish something. They are the negative considerations to which we agree that something cannot be done, the thoughts that stop you or your team from accomplishing your mission, or from attaining your goals. Limits lie within the subjective realm, not the physical. One person will look at a 5,000-foot cliff and say, "Wow! I wonder how quickly I can get to the top?" while another person will say, "Wow! That limits me from getting to where I want to go." So, you see, the cliff is *not* the limitation. It is the personal conviction that something can't be done.

Knowing this makes it easier to eradicate your own limits and those of your team members. Have the courage to shatter limits and start expressing how you can accomplish the tasks you need to fulfill – no matter what they may be. This takes faith and patience – both forms of courage. If the team has limits, find who within the team fuels such limits and work with them to see that they can be overcome. This will remove limitations from the group and cause a great thrust forward toward the attainment of the mission or goal.

Courage comes in many forms. Understand the direction you want your team members to go in and have the courage to provide the guidance needed, no matter what obstacles may be encountered. That's how the Marines have produced thousands upon thousands of leaders. That's how you can become a leader as well.

COMMITMENT

Commitment is a desire to be obligated to a cause or belief.

A committed leader is someone who will not give in to weakness and follow the path of least resistance. In the modern world it often seems easier to take shortcuts and quit when things become difficult. A committed leader does not do that. Commitment means sticking it out and working hard, staying the course until the mission has been accomplished or the goal has been achieved. Commitment displays intestinal fortitude. It demonstrates that one has the guts to do the right thing whether anyone is watching or not, or even when it is not popular.

Commitment is an awesome virtue. Just like the other core values we have discussed so far – honor and courage – commitment covers a broad spectrum of qualities and character traits that one needs in order to be a respected leader.

Do you work for the people who work for you? Are you committed to them? If not, then how can you expect them to be committed to you? Just because you're the boss or you cut the paychecks doesn't mean that commitment will be present. On the contrary. Commitment is the process of working through challenges and continuing to support your teammates in times of difficulty. Loyalty and respect are pathways to commitment and should be displayed to each other to keep unwanted friction from

65

slowing progress.

The "no retreat, no surrender" attitude that Marines display is the commitment they share for each other and the cause. Throughout history, everyone who has led a revolution has believed in a cause. They were passionate about a belief, and others observed their desire and integrity so they joined the cause. Committed people inspire others to believe. To be a true leader, you must inspire others by your obvious commitment.

Look at any company's turnover rate. Thousands of dollars are invested in the training and development of an individual. But often this money is squandered because the person grows frustrated and leaves the organization, and the whole cycle of training — money spent — employee frustration repeats itself. Why do people get frustrated? It's not because of what you might think – salary. Money is the often falsely assigned reason why people move on to other careers. However, the truth is that people want to advance. Everyone wants more responsibility and the ability to use their experience as time goes on. Pay is an incentive, not a motive. Money is secondary to the principle of growth. Employees want to be used to their fullest potential and paid for the results they produce. When you give an individual a chance to use all of their skills and work experience, they will become more committed to you and your team. The Marines know this to be true. Many a time, they have taken a person, trained them, and then allowed them to put all of their skills to work for the team. The person approaches the job with passion, honor, and yes, commitment. They do not want to let the other team members down.

Afterwards, with the task completed correctly, and if they are properly compensated, they demonstrate a renewed willingness to remain with the organization – as will your people. By simply putting your best people into the best positions to achieve results, you will have saved the organization you work for the thousands that they spent on recruiting and training, and preserved a valuable company asset. This is what a leader does.

Where is money in all of this? It certainly is a factor, but it is relatively low on the totem pole, certainly below having a position of potential advancement, beneath positions that allow worthy accomplishment, and in many cases below the motivation of duty—whether it be in the military or in the business world. Of course money is important and needed, but the point here is, once again, money is NOT "numero uno" like most managers imagine. It is an easily measurable fact that most people are not paid as much as they would like. Still, there are almost as many individuals who are quite fulfilled with their jobs – especially those who are led by great leaders.

Being committed, having courage, and maintaining a sense of duty works hand-in-hand with honor. They are tied together and strengthen each other in harmony. Marines develop and strengthen their core values in order to become better human beings. As a business leader, you can develop these characteristics in both yourself and others to become better people, better team members, and superior achievers.

Honor, courage, and commitment are core values in the Marine Corps. They are instilled into each Marine from the time he or she enters boot camp to the time he or she exits service. These three virtues are easy to study and implement. You should analyze these core values and incorporate them into your daily routine at work and at home. By internalizing (absorbing, assimilating, understanding) and then displaying these important attributes, you will aid yourself in being a leader, and you will aid yourself in your life.

‹◊› Chapter Four ‹◊›
Leadership Traits:
The DNA of Greatness

‹◊› Chapter Four ‹◊›

Leadership Traits:
The DNA of Greatness

*H*ow is leadership developed? What are some of the tools that a leader uses to become better? In this chapter we will answer these and other questions as we explore ourselves and our leadership capabilities by holding them up to standards. This is how new leaders are made and existing ones made even better.

Leadership can be acquired and molded by observation, experience, and emulation. Because "people management" is so difficult – no matter whether it's in the realm of the Marine Corps or the business world – an extremely useful exercise for leaders is to grade themselves on a monthly basis on the traits that affect them and their team members the most. The Marine Corps has used this grading technique for years, and swears by it. It has molded men and women from the furnace of adversity into the cold, hardened steel of leaders, and it can do the same for you. Every leader in the Corps receives a report card on how they did over a certain period of time. This report card is based on the fourteen leadership characteristics, which are known by the acronym JJ DID TIE BUCKLE. (We will cover this in more detail in Chapter 6: Leadership Counseling.)

It was humid on Paris Island in July. For me, the culture shock of boot camp was starting to wear off. The long days of receiving (the first few days of boot camp) were gone and training had commenced. I fought through the fog of exhaustion and itch of sand flea bites in order to truly understand through hands-on experience, what was being taught by my leaders – not just glibly receive the information. My drill instructors had me yelling the acronym "JJ DID TIE BUCKLE" at the top of my lungs until I saw those words in my sleep. The larger-than-life leaders gave my fellow recruits and me many classes on what each word means to them and how it applies to a combat situation. We would repeat the words over and over:

"SIR, THE FOURTEEN LEADERSHIP TRAITS ARE: JJ DID TIE BUCKLE, [meaning] JUDGMENT, JUSTICE, DEPENDABILITY, INTEGRITY, DECISIVENESS, TACT, ENTHUSIASM, BEARING, UNSELFISHNESS, COURAGE, KNOWLEDGE, LOYALTY, AND ENDURANCE – DONE SIR, DONE!" My throat would burn from the long duration of the ditty but when each word was screamed in unison with the recruit to the left or right of me, the display of teamwork would please the drill instructors and therefore make us proud. The minor discomfort in my throat was an acceptable sacrifice for the team known as Platoon 3139. It was obvious that Marines not only understood leadership, they applied it in their character. Each trait to a Marine is a gem in a treasure box of virtues that combine to make the professional reputation of the United States Marine Corps.

After you become more experienced and settled in the Corps your study of leadership becomes more and more intense. The purpose for these studies is to aid us in advancing and leading more Marines. The best part is that our personal growth doesn't stop and it is evident in the most peculiar experiences.

I remember driving to Virginia to link up with the rest of my Marines at Virginia Beach when traffic started to slow. As we negotiated through the congestion we came upon an accident. There were no first responders on the scene yet, such as police, firemen, or EMS. We decided to act.

We began to help direct traffic and provide first aid. There was only one other gentleman helping at the scene. He was controlling the flow of everything, like an on-scene commander. He was dressed casually, yet was obviously in charge. He directed and organized us as we waited for the highway patrol to arrive. I walked over and asked if he was a policeman or EMS and he shook his head with a smile. No, he was a former Marine, just helping out by taking initiative. He was performing just the way Marines do – working hard to do the right thing.

I'd like to think that this defines Marine initiative – taking charge and offering assistance without being asked simply because it is the right thing to do.

It quickly became evident to me that, from our intense beginning at boot camp until the day we retire, the fourteen leadership traits are the DNA for designing and developing a more fulfilling life. They can certainly help you in business leadership as well.

We will now examine each of these fourteen characteristics. Take note as to how many of these traits you can honestly say you possess. What traits are you good at? Which ones do you need to incorporate into your leadership model?

JUDGMENT

In any position of responsibility, a leader must exercise sound judgment. Take time to weigh your options before you decide, and try to choose the best course of action for the situation at the time. Do not settle for the minimum. Try to make the best decisions, and move on.

JUSTICE

Be fair in your actions. Show equity and do not create favorites in the group. Justice is blind and people deserve honest and balanced consequences. Your team members deserve nothing less. Reward the willing and encourage the wayward. Don't give your team members any reason to try any less than you.

DEPENDABILITY

Make sure personally that your tasks are completed

in a timely fashion. Supervise your people and hold them accountable to the timelines you have laid out according to the dictates of the task or goal. Demonstrate dependability and let your team know that you can be trusted with any job. Your reputation will supersede any complaints from negative co-workers or subordinates. Let the sheer power of these traits start to work for you so that they positively influence every work situation.

INTEGRITY

Integrity is being honest to yourself and honest to others. It is being morally upright. Never compromise your word — never, never, never. Hold fast the duties that you openly accept in earnest, and fulfill all promises made. Your integrity in every situation is critical. If someone is not up to the standards you have set for the team, and that other members are achieving, let them know. By the same token, if someone is operating beyond expectations, let them know. Let your word be an absolute bond that your team can trust implicitly. Live, eat, and sleep integrity in all that you do. If you do this, you will soon find that living by integrity will aid you in every aspect of your life.

DECISIVENESS

When the clock is running it is better to make a wrong decision than none at all. Your team looks to you for decisions, answers, guidance – so supply them swiftly and assuredly. Use all the data you have available to you and decide upon a course of action, and then stick to the plan.

You may troubleshoot the plan as required, but believe in each decision that you make and let it unfold accordingly. If something more ideal is revealed as things are lived out, don't be bullheaded or embarrassed. Make the appropriate adjustments and get on with it.

TACT

Treat higher and lower management personnel with equal respect and humility. Just because someone is lower than you in the organizational pecking order doesn't mean that they deserve the brush-off or disrespect. Speak to everyone the way you would want to be spoken to. You can be firm with people and still be fair; treat everyone you come in contact with like an adult. In the Marine Corps, the instructors and leaders may seem hard on recruits sometimes, but they are never disrespectful toward them. Even the person of the lowest rank is treated with respect.

INITIATIVE

Devise and then implement ways to make your team more efficient on a consistent basis — **without** being told to do so. Seize the moment, take initiative and make things happen yourself, without being ordered to do so. Don't bypass someone else's job or wreak havoc by not following the initialized plan, but know what your duties and responsibilities are and act independently to get them done. Acting independently may or may not include doing something alone. If a task requires more than one person to accomplish, take the personal initiative to get it started by pulling together the necessary personnel, equipment, and so forth. Streamline and organize your work load by operating in your scope of authority. Co-workers will observe how well your shop is doing and they will take the initiative to streamline theirs. Nothing is copied more than success! This explains, in part, why the Marine Corps is one of the most duplicated armed forces units in the world.

This is no boasting, it is simply a fact that Marines have led the way as an expeditionary fighting force almost since its inception. The official mission is to be a force in readiness; therefore, Marine leadership has been at the forefront in anticipating change and meeting such volatile demands with effective measures that stabilize and neutralize as needed. This is the type of initiative leaders must sometimes take. Marines have taken the initiative on many things, from changing the military fighting uniform to developing a cutting-edge martial arts program, to name a couple. We didn't wait to be asked; we did it because it was the right thing to do.

This is initiative. And it is what you should readily demonstrate as a leader. Don't wait to be asked; if it's the right thing to do — do it.

ENTHUSIASM

Demonstrate how motivated you are to the cause, then watch your enthusiasm spread among your team members. Morale is a virus that spreads faster than any words ever could. Accept adversity and challenge with gusto. Show your excitement about the projects you undergo. Possessing and displaying a positive attitude can uplift a person, section, shop, company..., faster than words.

BEARING

Never lose your composure under pressure. Keep your cool in times of crisis and/or challenge and focus on results during critical times. Clear your mind and solve problems using logic, not emotion or reaction. A leader is not defined by his or her actions when times are easy. They are rather discovered by what they do when situations are challenging. As the old maxim says: "When the going gets tough, the tough get going."

UNSELFISHNESS

Operate without selfish motive or intentions. Do not try to benefit yourself by working towards building your own empire. People are watching you and your actions. Be a true team player and make sacrifices for the greater cause of the team. Glory hounds come and go. They don't last because people see through their masked intentions of personal gain, And there are far, far more real leaders than there are glory hounds.

COURAGE

We've covered this before, but it bears extension here: Beyond overcoming adversity and standing up to one's fears, have the moral courage to do the right thing, whether someone is watching or you're alone. Be your own conscience, be your best counsel. Be proud of who looks back at you in the mirror.

KNOWLEDGE

Know your job and what is expected from you and your subordinates. Understand what you're doing and the purpose for your efforts. Nothing is worse than having a leader talk about something with obvious ignorance. Never "wing" anything, meaning don't try to pretend to know the answer and dazzle your teammates and others with false verbosity. Research and study will save you the embarrassment of appearing as a fool. Negative impressions are difficult to erase. If you don't know something, don't rattle off a potentially wrong answer. This can put everyone, and the cause, at unnecessary risk. Instead, find out the truth about it and share it with the others. Experience is your best teacher. Realize that textbook or verbal education is not all that you need to know. Data alone are only concepts awaiting application. New ideas and plans on paper are only that, and they are unproven. And not until you've tried the data out, until you have tested the ideas and plans, will you come to truly know about those things. Data can't be swung like a sword. Information cannot even be used as a doorstop. Experience is king; that's when real understanding is achieved. The moral: don't think you know it all just because you've read about it in an article or book or "studied" it in a course room. Learn about your post and the posts of your subordinates. "Know" what you and your teammates are supposed to "do." If it's an action, then practice it, drill it – move it over from information to experience. If you need to know about a widget, if you're going to be handling one, you better not be satisfied with just a description of it. Find one, look at it, feel it in your hands, smell it, learn how it works and work it. Then you will have real knowledge of your and your subordinates' post duties and equipment.

LOYALTY

Show your loyalty to your team and to your higher management. Not everyone agrees on everything, but working together and staying focused on the task at hand creates unit cohesion. Remember that a unit as a whole is stronger than a group of individuals. Can your teammates count on you? Do they know that you will be there for them for the necessary support and guidance? Do you have greater interests elsewhere that supersede your team? This never goes unnoticed; they will feel it. You must be committed to your team and they will be committed to the cause. You cannot be a half-hearted leader of anything. It's all or nothing. You're either in or you step down. A leader is the focal point, the source of energy, the catalyst of inspiration. And a team is the mirror image of what their leader does or doesn't do for them. Be dependable, be loyal and allegiance will grow and not wander.

ENDURANCE

Show the determination to stick it out to the finish. Make a pact with yourself and your team members to bring the plan through to completion, to attainment. Throwing in the towel is giving up, a form of losing. Develop and exhibit the physical endurance and mental fortitude to complete and accomplish any and all tasks. THAT is a winning proposition!

Take a piece of paper and write down the acronym JJ DID TIE BUCKLE and clear your mind. It's time for you to accurately and fairly grade yourself on these characteristics we've just gone over. It goes without saying that you should have the integrity to grade yourself in earnest and without reasonableness or exceptions. This is one of the most important report cards you will ever receive because it's not about math or science. It is about you. And the more honest you are with yourself, the more you will get out of this potentially life-changing action. No one else will review this report card but you. And it will go a long way toward helping you inwardly become the person and leader you want to be.

Rate yourself on each characteristic by assigning a number from 1-10: with 1 representing the poorest example of it and 10 representing the greatest example. Remember, don't be reasonable or make excuses. Score yourself in an unbiased manner. The success of this vital action relies completely on your honesty.

All right, let's see how you did. Do you have many 5s? Any 4s? How about 2s or 1s? Don't worry, this action isn't for ridicule or scorn. It is for you to realize a starting point from which you can now improve.

Take note of your areas of strength – those would be the ones with 7s or better. In general, we can agree that we all have room for improvement. And it is from this stance that we begin to work on these points. If you've done this correctly and honestly, your strengths and weaknesses should jump out at you. Leaders must seek self-improvement on a continual basis. This is because our constant striving for personal perfection will make us better and better leaders. And our improvements will reap more and more successes, not to mention our own efforts in setting a great example to the team members, who will begin to seek such personal improvement. Why are these fourteen points so very important? Because without ALL of them in a healthy range the leader suffers. More precisely, the degree that these points are weak or nonexistent is the degree to which one will fail at leading others.

We can, for the sake of this topic, compare a leader to an engine in a machine. Finely tuned, with all of its parts clean and running at peak levels and all properly aligned, the engine can run faster and farther, allowing the machine to produce more and take the team to greater heights and further distances. The better the engine runs, the greater the successes. On the other hand, an engine put together with dirty, worn parts – even some missing pieces – the antithesis occurs and the poorer the engine runs, the less desirable achievements happens. Other parts of the machine break and become misaligned, and the machine eventually breaks down if the engine is in poor enough shape.

It is not necessary for every one of the fourteen points to be at 7 or above to become a leader. What is necessary is that you, as a leader, begin to relentlessly strive for greater personal excellence in all leadership points from here on out. In doing so, you will be able to deal with any situation or circumstance life can throw at you. And you and your team will thrive.

Having the ability to change your tactics and adapt to different situations is key for leadership success. When you monitor your leadership abilities and continually improve, you will inevitably produce a higher quality individual in yourself and a higher quality individual produces higher quality work and a higher quality team.

The Marine Corps has been character building for hundreds of years. We build character by constantly monitoring ourselves in an honest and forthright manner. The Corps teaches that we can, and must always aspire to, improve, every day in every way. It may be a long journey and it may never end. But you are always trying to improve, and that is the point of importance being asserted here.

Do you think that this is an empty exercise, that trying to make yourself a better person and a better leader is not something that you should constantly strive for? If so, I'd like to share another anecdote with you:

Private Johnny was a non-athletic character with no sense of humor. He was a skinny runt from Oklahoma who had trouble fitting in at school, let alone the green machine known as the United States Marine Corps.

When I first encountered him he had been picked on, isolated, and forgotten. His personal finances were in shambles and his personality was nothing to be desired.

Johnny had trouble with simple tasks, such as making his bed. His personal hygiene and physical fitness were a disgrace. He never stood up for himself.

My plan was simple: never stop trying to improve and never leave a Marine – or a fellow human being – behind. I helped him create a budget for his finances. I demonstrated how to make a bed to my standards, then ripped the sheets off and let him start from scratch. It was odd to teach a grown man how to brush his teeth, but I did it. He went on runs with me to improve his physical confidence. Gradually the skinny Oklahoma kid became a man. Every day in every way he became better. Besides self-improvement, there was an urgency behind my efforts. An Iraq deployment was in the near future and since anything is possible in combat, he had to become strong.

After a few months of this type of routine I would inspect his small tasks. He was held accountable on days he did not meet expectations and rewarded with a pat on the back on the days he did.

Then he was sent to Iraq. Had my efforts been enough? Had Johnny improved enough to not be a danger to himself or others?

During operation Iraqi Freedom, Johnny led over fifty combat scouting patrols. He advised his section leader on the best routes to use due to his vast understanding of the routes he had patrolled. He identified five improvised explosive devices (roadside bombs) on his route reconnaissance patrols and had them neutralized so they wouldn't kill another civilian or fellow Marine. This is just a small list of his many accomplishments. The bottom line was that Johnny was able to save many lives, including his own.

The skinny runt from Oklahoma had done a complete 180 degree turnaround. Johnny was honored by those who served with him during these operations. He earned the respect he deserved and became a better person because he applied what he had learned. His life was altered because of Marine Corps leadership.

Every day, in every way, he got better. Men and women are alive today who may not have been if not for Johnny's leadership skills.

To allow the leadership traits and principles we've discussed in this chapter to work for you means sacrifice – but they are worth it. Take sincere interest in becoming a better leader and a better human being. Give up the concept of "self" and become a juggernaut for the loyal people who support you. You in turn will be more satisfied with your work environment and family life.

Who knows, you might even save a life.

◄◇► Chapter Five ◄◇►
Leadership Principles

⟨◇⟩ Chapter Five ⟨◇⟩
Leadership Principles

*T*his chapter will help propel you further toward the goal of leadership by discussing the principles of leadership. Leadership principles are key to developing leaders. They are laws that enable anyone to move ever closer to leadership attainment—the bullets that streak toward the bull's eye in the middle of the target. They are also fundamental ideals that the Corps follows every day to help mold leaders out of followers.

Great leadership is not easy; it requires work, training and confront. The good news is, however, that if you continuously strive to improve – and just by using this book you are doing so—you will reach your full leadership potential.

Countless men and women in the Marine Corps have felt the sinking feeling of despair; those sometimes overwhelming, always negative thoughts of "can't do" that we all have felt at one time or another. It is not uncommon to experience temporary emotions of doubt and uncertainty when faced with something we've yet to prove to ourselves that we actually "can do." And attaining the status of a leader of a group – a position that requires full responsibility for not only success of the established plan but the immediate well-being of others – can certainly appear to be beyond one's capabilities at first glance. But even at that moment when you stand and stare into the daunting abyss of potential failure without retreat, it means that you are trying to improve and determined to succeed. And such an acknowledgement to yourself that "confronting is improving" enforces your resolve to face the unknown, overcome fear, and become stronger and better. As the message in this book has stressed, you have to believe in yourself first before anybody else will. Don't disqualify yourself as a leader if you ever feel doubt. That is just a normal human reaction. Just recognize that the simple act of doubting and then wanting to overcome that doubt means you have the spark and inner fire so necessary for being a good leader. The correct thing to do is congratulate yourself for conquering the major hurdles of personal sabotage.

In the Corps in the year 2005, the Javelin section of the Combined Anti-Armor team had a Sergeant who micro-managed every task assigned to his unit. Much like a dictator, his obsessive need to control weighed heavy on each member of the team. The unit's proficiency was at an all-time low, because its members relied solely on this individual for solutions. This section had the most disciplinary issues in the platoon, marksmanship was below standard, physical fitness flew out the window, and morale was absent without leave. At this point in time these Marines had not been trained in leadership or their infantry skills – a circumstance that can get many Marines killed.

Sensing trouble, the Platoon Commander identified the need for instilling and delegating leadership, and suggested that I become their section leader. But there was the problem that I was not a Javelin, meaning that I had not gone to school and learned the job designation that was needed to lead this team in combat. This unit was trained to handle the Javelin weapon system, which is essentially a missile launching system. But one characteristic of a good leader is stretching his or her limits, being willing to do something never done before. I wanted to challenge my versatility and demonstrate to the subordinates a loyalty to them, so I decided to learn the trade inside-out – much better than their previous leader. Knowing myself and seeking self-improvement are two leadership traits that I had to execute to be considered a sincere leader and not just a politician stepping into a position. (Knowing yourself and seeking self-improvement will be elaborated on as we continue through this book.)

After developing a complete understanding of the operations and capabilities of the Javelin weapon system and the employment of its Marines, my next challenge was to incorporate leadership education to the Javelin subordinates. A training schedule was created to not only train for combat but develop leaders amongst the section. Special attention was given to the Javelin Team Leaders in order to bring them to standard. We started to critique and document each other's progress, and they started to demonstrate professionalism and ethics. To my surprise, in a relatively short time they went from worst to first!

This change did not occur because of my need for control but rather because I delegated authority and relied heavily on my Team Leaders. The Team Leaders made it possible to be the best by harnessing the frustration of the others and enjoying the freedom to execute orders without someone constantly looking over their shoulders. Without the restraints of micro-managing they executed flawlessly and their pride in the team reflected a disciplined and professional attitude.

This just goes to show that leadership doesn't take an overbearing, in-your-face approach. Find your leaders, delegate authority, then stand back and watch them execute. The Corps thrives on this type of action. Whether in yourself or in others, develop leaders, not followers.

The 11 Leadership Principles

There are 11 principles that define leadership:

1. Know yourself and seek self-improvement.

How many times have you heard this already? Yet it bears repeating, because this is the most important of all leadership principles. Once you set this first one in motion you can start working on all the rest. Can you see how it works? Visualize, if you will, the questions asked thus far. They lead to a better understanding of yourself. Look at how seeking self-improvement actually affects your life and the lives of others. You become not just a superior leader, but a better spouse, parent, neighbor, and friend. Perhaps you even become a pillar of your community – someone to be called upon in times of need. It is no accident that the people others often rely on are military personnel, and even more often Marines. They have the art of self-improvement etched in their DNA. And in other less drastic times, as upstanding persons in a community they are called upon, often on a somewhat regular basis. To say the least, helping is rewarding.

So try to consistently evolve to become a more efficient and effective leader. Acknowledge friction and understand that, as a leader, you must provide a solution. Once that solution is devised and put into action, you should be able to see the problem resolve. If not, have the flexibility and ingenuity to develop another solution. Blind stubbornness is a fool's virtue. Once the problem is resolved do not dwell on it, but move on to yet greater tasks to accomplish, creating larger and larger effects. When you apply this most fundamental of all leadership principles, "mission accomplished" becomes a result – not a focus – and you have the platform for becoming an exceptional leader.

2. Be technically and tactically proficient.

Understand your role as a leader as well as what is expected from your people so that you can employ them properly. Demonstrating your ability to execute sound technical and tactical skill provides subordinates with the confidence in you to lead them effectively. Remember, meeting the goal is the minimum that should be expected and anticipated; going beyond could well reap untold benefits. You do that by being technically and tactically proficient in every facet of your job, for you never know when a skill or scrap of information is going to be required. By allowing your leadership skills to work for you, your work load will shift and become easier and more fun. This happens by being technically and tactically proficient. When you understand and know how to use the technical and leadership skills you possess, the arrow of proficiency increases and advancements – professional and personal – come naturally.

3. Develop a sense of responsibility amongst your subordinates.

Every member of your team plays a vital role in achieving the ultimate goal. Show them the role they play, and make them understand how important the work they perform is to the team. Make them understand that without their part the team would have a much tougher time completing its mission – because it's the truth. When all parts work together as one, great things happen. Thus, when a teammate feels they have a responsibility to you or the team they put more effort into their work. It is your job to let them know they are important.

4. Make sound and timely decisions.

Procrastination, and then implementing plans that display minimum thought, demonstrate lack of attention to detail. Believe me, that sort of thing is noticed by your superiors. It certainly is here in the Marine Corps, with the result that the leader who submits them – you – is diminished in everyone's eyes. The way to avoid this is to hold yourself accountable to time limits and plan accordingly. Meet or beat those time limits if possible with a plan that goes beyond what is called for, and demonstrates drive and initiative. Then keep the momentum going and stay on track. Think of your plans as a train taking you to your destination. The train can function very easily when on track – when its plan allows it to move smoothly. However, once the train derails – once the plans are either not available or hastily-conceived – it is a nightmare to get it going again.

5. Set the ideal example.

You, as the leader, are under constant scrutiny. It is your duty to not just set **an** example, but set **the** example. When you do so your team members have the perfect standard to follow. Do you remember the expression "do as I say, not as I do"? Well, forget it, because following that advice is a terrible blunder. Your team looks up to you and will naturally follow your actions. Make sure they are actions worth following. Never act as if rules apply any differently to you because you are the boss.

6. Know your team and look after their welfare.

You are the one who has to oversee the well-being of your team. This doesn't mean calling every night to make certain that they get home safely, but rather, assuring that you do all you can to make their work experience a pleasant and stress-free environment. People work best when they can focus on the task at hand. So you must monitor your team, and have your radar attuned to things that may be wrong. After all, how effective would a squad of Marines be if they had their minds elsewhere when they were supposed to be performing a mission? So learn to give and accept feedback. Most people will work even when they are sick because of fear of being labeled a malingerer, so it is up to you to be aware that something is wrong and make a decision as to whether or not it could affect the team as a whole. Know when something is wrong and take care of your people. Do not lead blindly, and pay attention to how your folks operate. Do not just take someone else's word that "everything is fine" because they may be trying to hide a problem out of friendship or misguided loyalty. A Marine leader's very life may depend on how his or her unit is functioning, so taking things for granted is not an option, neither for them nor for you. Get down in the trenches with your people and find out how they operate when they are feeling fine. That way you'll be more aware when something is wrong, just like a race car driver knows from the sound of his/her engine if it's all right or not.

7. Keep your team informed.

It creates unnecessary friction when your team does not know what is going on. Become the public information officer for your group. Hold meetings and review statistics and topics that need to be addressed. Print a newsletter that keeps people informed of the company's activities, and how it impacts their work. Get the word out and then ask every person if they understand it. If not, repeat it until it is understood. Supervise the chain of communication, and immediately repair broken links when necessary.

8. Seek responsibility and take responsibility for your action.

Isn't it amazing how many managers unfairly place blame on their subordinates? Resist doing this with every fiber of your being, for it breeds only resentment and hostility among your team members. It is human nature to want to shift the blame to someone else on the team because it keeps you from appearing in a negative light. Ultimately, however, leaders can delegate authority but not responsibility. When something on your plan fails, accept the responsibility and provide a solution to correct the problem. Every person makes mistakes — shrug it off and be thick-skinned.

To put it another way, how many Marines would be willing to come to the aid of a back-stabbing leader? Wouldn't it be human nature to want to watch the leader fail? That's why a Marine leader CANNOT afford to blame others for his or her mistakes. The next time that that leader needs the help of a team member may be a life-or-death situation. Simmering resentments aren't very good life-savers.

Look to assume new tasks and help other departments if things are running smoothly with your team. It is amazing to see how grateful people are for just receiving a simple helping hand. (There may be a day when you need one as well, so piling up "owe you ones" does not hurt.) Do not show off and perform tasks for self-benefit. By the same token, do not overwork your team solely for your own glory. If your goal is met can you aid someone who is running behind just to help them out? (Not only will doing so accumulate I.O.U.'s. but it will make you feel better about yourself as a person, and that's part and parcel of becoming a good leader.) Do not do their job for them, but aid with simple tasks to help. It can mean a world of difference.

9. Ensure that tasks are understood, supervised, and accomplished.

When it comes to assigning tasks, first and foremost, make sure that you know what the overall goal is. There has to be good communication above and below your level of command. Make sure you know what the higher-ups want to achieve. There's nothing more destructive and dangerous than a misinformed team unwittingly working against the intentions of management. Then let your men know.

Set targets higher than what is needed or being

asked for. Mankind would have never reached the moon if it did not first reach for the stars. As a down-to-Earth description of this, with the unforeseen and foreseen opposing forces that we experience in day-to-day life, it is only logical and essential that we go for more than the desired, intended result just in order to attain that result. If it is time-related, establish a faster/earlier time for completion, if that timeline is "at all" possible. If the goal is quantitative, set it ten, twenty, thirty percent higher than what is needed or demanded.

When you assign a task, ask if there are any questions. Do not assume your people understand what you assign, no matter how simple it appears to be. Review everyone's comprehension by quizzing them after you delegate the task. Have them explain the plan back to you. This is called Back Briefing. As you can imagine, it is critical for a Marine to understand his or her mission. Even a training exercise can go horribly wrong if not understood by everyone. Back Briefing has saved many a mission. It can do the same for you in the business world by saving a valuable client or even the company as a whole.

Once the task has been assigned, periodically check the quality of your team's work. Note whether they are on schedule for meeting a certain timeline. Let them know if they are behind but don't bypass them by taking over. Has what they've achieved so far been done correctly for allowing the desired result to come through? Review what has been accomplished, correct if correction is needed, but do not interfere with progress. Ideally, you will have properly explained what is needed and made sure that each person knows and can do their job. And you will essentially be invisible so that your people can operate without the pressure of the boss interfering with their assigned tasks that they themselves need to complete if they are to perceive themselves to have any worth to the team.

"Supervise" the task from development to completion, don't take over. An inability to delegate responsibility and invest trust in one's team members is a serious flaw. Supervising, directing, giving orders, guiding are your responsibility. But very importantly, let your team do their job. That is what a good leader does.

10. Train your employees as a team.

The importance of team dynamics is fundamental to any type of work, in any environment at any time. It is paramount. Five people have more energy than one. A chain is only as strong as its weakest link. You've heard the clichés, but I'm here to tell you that in the Marine Corps you quickly find out that these aren't clichés. They are valuable truths — maxims to win by.

Part of the process of growth and improvement in your team is the working together, working out the conflicts of personality, learning to work in unison, like a machine. Equity, balance, camaraderie, communication... are not taught as much as they are developed through the evolutionary growth of a team that trains together. Let them know they are not a bunch of individuals, but something much greater as a whole.

11. Employ your group in accordance with its capabilities.

Every person has a strength or level of expertise that they bring to the table. Identify these strengths and abilities of each individual and incorporate tasks that best suit them. Use your team's strengths to cover gaps in capability and spread the work out. This prevents friction and keeps people feeling confident. Do not over-task, yet do not fail to challenge each team member. This means that some will have more to do or will have to handle more difficult tasks than others. Never expect everyone to possess equal strength and ability, but relentlessly encourage personal improvement, strive for personal bests, and seek utmost capability in everyone. Meet any sluggards with discipline, but be sure not to confuse inability or lack of experience for laziness. Accomplishment refines itself when the art of leadership is used on a mission in the Marine Corps by using people's strengths and weaknesses.

The scope of leadership traits and principles ranges from broad to narrow. Leadership is a progressive art that needs constant study. It is also a craft in which its skills need continuous honing. But if you use these 11 leadership principles, you will be certain to go a long way toward becoming the kind of leader men and women can look up to and emulate. And you will create big effects. I know this firsthand; I've seen it happen time and again in the Marine Corps. And now it can happen for you. ◄◊►

◄◊► Chapter Six ◄◊►
Leadership Counseling

◄◊► Chapter Six ◄◊►
Leadership Counseling

*D*o you want to know how your people are doing, how they're holding up under the pressures and demands? Of course you do, and that's a good quality to have. A leader must be concerned about the ones he or she leads. For all of the Hollywood movies about tough military drill instructors, it is a fact that every D.I. cares about the welfare of the people being instructed. As a leader in the business world, you need to care about the folks who are working for you. There is obviously more to this or else there would be no need for a chapter by itself. This has to do with something that can't be learned as much as brought forth from within, maintained, or strengthened.

It is worthwhile, due to witnessing the improper handling of people all too often, to state here that no matter what the arrangement is – under contract or under duty or otherwise – there is no good reason not to be genuinely concerned about the well-being of every one of your team members. Don't get caught in making excuses why you don't have to care. Shallow and single-minded considerations like "They get paid well," or "They knew the circumstances before they arrived," are no excuses to treat people like they are less than human.

One might think there's no time for this with all the work there is to get done. But it's easy to do: you simply ask them how they are doing on a regular basis. The essence and value of this has to do with "genuinely" caring. Going through the motions won't cut it, as your people will feel the insincerity and will be invalidated by it. The old saying 'you get what you give' is never more appropriate than here. If you don't care about your subordinates, they won't care about you. This will fester negativity and eventually break up the team one way or another, not before experiencing much unnecessary strife and extra toil, and the whole company will suffer.

This doesn't mean that you have to pacify or baby people. Nor does it mean you should not expect, even demand, excellence and the most from your people. It simply means what it means: sincerely caring for others.

Make it a priority to set aside time to have them discuss any concerns or opinions they may have about you, the task, the company…anything they have their mind on.

Marine Non-Commissioned Officers perform monthly counseling for their subordinates to gauge the performance of every Marine. Counseling is done from a sit-down mentoring standpoint and acts as a guideline for junior Marines to meet senior Marine expectations and instructions. The leader provides insight into the negative and positive behaviors displayed throughout the counseling dialogue. In order to give the subordinate some possible solutions to increase performance, they cooperate on specifying the direction and behaviors displayed throughout the period assigned for that counseling. Guidance for any personal or professional goal is offered and documented by the senior officer. Counseling also assesses the junior Marine's past performance to verify his or her ability to meet necessary goals. Face to face with the junior Marine, the senior officer/leader discusses that soldier's strengths and weaknesses, and assigns tasks to be completed by the junior Marine before the next counseling session. This is an easily-implemented technique that can produce amazing results.

Every human being wants to do better, and desires recognition for doing so. If you tap into that individual's goals and set a structure for the direction you want them to head, then your team will be more efficient and time will be saved.

If a team member does not understand what is expected from him/her, then there is a vagueness to his or her understanding of how to benefit the company. This, among other things, is like having a cylinder unplugged from an engine. That person's capabilities and power are barely being utilized. And in most cases, this person will do things opposite to the direction and intentions of the group. As a leader, it is your job to help each member clearly understand their purpose, their goal, their job — what they are being relied on by everyone else to do. Set simple yet obtainable goals that best suit the individual's capabilities. Setting your employees up for success is your responsibility.

If you are the leader of a large organization, try implementing guidance on a monthly basis for division heads and have them filter it down the chain of command. Productivity increases because understanding increases and camaraderie grows. The guidance can be as simple and informal as pulling them aside on a regular basis. If they have the drive to succeed, give them the tools and show them the way.

Every team member has virtues that they want to have recognized and appreciated. The monthly review is a way to remind them of what they are doing well and what they need to correct. Notice that this is not just a faultfinding process. There is a balance of acknowledging the good and helping to eliminate the errors. Understand that, though they may not have any authority to openly grade your performance, if you are watching for their values, they will be watching for yours. Once again, you are setting an example. This is why we repeatedly stress the importance of knowing yourself and seeking self-improvement. You have read this aspect more than anything else in this book. It is because of its immense importance. And as you appraise your team, take a second and honestly examine yourself. Look at your virtues and critique yourself the same way you would your own team members. What do you discover?

METHODS

As noted above, counseling plays an extremely important part in leadership. There are three types of counseling methods that the Marine Corps uses to obtain excellent results: Formal, Informal, and On-The-Spot. Let's discuss each of these three methods below:

Formal Counseling

This method consists of holding an assigned session between the leader and the employee. Formal methods are more disciplinary in nature than other methods. The leader conducts the counseling, guiding the individual with specific goals based upon the leader's perception of how the employee is performing.

If you are going to utilize this method, make certain you take time to prepare before starting the session. Have the necessary documentation ready in a drawer or similar private setting in order to keep the focus on the topics being covered, but so it's available if needed.

Informal Counseling

The Informal Counseling method is most effective when used in a frequent and timely manner. For example, this method could be used if a major positive goal has been met or if it has not been reached. Another example of when it could be used would be if an individual continued to display atypical performance.

When used on a regular basis – say monthly – the informal method can help direct or redirect a team member. Remember to keep the sessions constructive. If no redirection is needed, these sessions can be used to reassure an individual about their performance. Informal sessions motivate team members continuously. The beauty of such sessions is that they can correct or rectify a situation before it mushrooms and requires more formal counseling.

On-the-Spot Counseling

This method, the most informal of the three, corrects deficiencies and implements changes immediately when the need for such is noted.

We have just covered the three methods for effective counseling. A good leader utilizes not just one of these, but all three, picking the most appropriate depending upon the situation.

When you utilize any of these counseling methods, there are three different approaches to use. I'll describe each approach below, and, like the counseling styles, you pick the one that is most appropriate. The three approaches are: directive, non-directive and a combination of the two.

Directive

With the Directive approach, you, as the leader, take charge. You decide the team member's problem(s). You provide solutions and/or consequences if the situation does not get resolved. This approach is best used in conjunction with formal counseling when there is a disciplinary issue that needs to be corrected.

Non-directive

In the Non-directive approach, you as leader, stress your belief in the team member's ability to identify and solve their problem by him/herself. Thus you make it clear that the responsibility for solving the problem rests on the team member. This approach is best used with the informal method of counseling, and is more suited to a mature employee because they tend to be more aware of goals, expectations, and the utilization of their own abilities.

Combination

The Combination approach is exactly what it sounds like: it uses elements from both the Directive and Non-directive approaches. Another term for it could be "Collaboration." Here, the leader and team member both exchange ideas, so the dialogue is very much a two-way street. You, as leader, would state the problem to the team member and guide him/her to come up with a solution rather than resolving it for them or having them figure it out all on their own.

There is no set format or formula of when to use a specific method or approach. Guiding and correcting is a cognitive tool that comes from experience and understanding how your employees react to different dialogues and methods. Some individuals might like more guidance. Others will appreciate resolving things single-handedly. Still others may desire being told what to do in order to make things right. A leader will find out, over time, what works best for each member. And with the ones who prefer that guidance or complete control be run on them, a good leader will slowly bring them toward greater independence and help them increase their personal responsibility levels. The majority of the time employees do not even know what they are doing that is slowing down progress or creating a problem. Counseling, which includes good communication skills and much listening on the leader's part, enables you to quickly identify friction points and bring these things to light to your subordinates so they can be corrected, adjusted, eliminated, or augmented.

Once again, you are strongly urged to come to know yourself and seek self-improvement, in this case, with regard to counseling. Why? Because counseling can be a double-edged sword and it can have an impact – positive or negative – on the results of your counsel. Look at how you counsel, and note the type of approach that you use on someone. Observe the effect you caused on that person. Did the person show good indications or bad? Meaning, did he/she come in looking bright and chipper but leave down in the dumps? More importantly, did they find a remedy or move towards improving the situation? Obviously, each employee responds better to a different type of counseling. Learning which methods work best on each member and honing your counsel will eventually create an efficient and winning approach to improving member performance, not to mention the priceless commodity of morale. These basic rules will aid any leader when addressing problems. Review your counseling to examine a team member's progress. Look at what approach worked and what approach missed the mark. Take note what approach works so you can utilize it the next time.

Remember, counseling has been tried and tested many times over by the Marine Corps. So nothing you get here or elsewhere in this book is extrapolation or theory. Some of the finest leaders in the business world have come out of the Marines, honed as leaders by these very techniques. They are proven and have stood the test of time. On a personal note, remember that story I told about myself as a wayward kid in the opening pages of this book? I am what I am today – a leader of men and women – because of these techniques and methods.

How well I remember, as if it were yesterday, stepping off of the bus and onto the barracks of the 3rd Battalion, 6th Marines, so many years ago. That world, at that moment, was as foreign to me as all of the countries I subsequently journeyed to during my career. Not knowing what to expect from my comrades or my leaders, I trusted in the discipline I learned in boot camp. Being motivated and extremely eager to learn had focused me to do a good job for the individual that would ultimately lay the foundation of my leadership. I listened sharply to every bit of advice from my senior Marines in order to calm the confusion that was growing inside of me.

Corporal Amaro, my squad leader, was directly responsible for my welfare and from my standpoint appeared to know everything about the Marine Corps. He was a great confidence-booster because he himself showed strong confidence, mixed with an easy-to-approach attitude to us new guys. He gave me about four working days to adjust to my surroundings and then began initial counseling with me. This counseling covered what was expected from me and went over the do's and don'ts around the camp. This meeting was a valuable asset; it kept me grounded and on the right path. It created more certainty in what I was supposed to do and further counseling enabled me to advance quickly by following his expert guidance.

After a year of development with the Marine Corps counseling system, Corporal Amaro was officially my mentor. As such, he made the decision to place me in a Meritorious Corporal Board where Lance Corporals compete against the best of their peers in a battalion competition. I won, and did so easily, solely because Corporal Amaro's standards were so incredibly high, yet his simple guidance acted as a passable road map to ease my way to success. It was a sweet victory. I rejoiced in my newfound respect for the counseling tool. The great behavioral rewards of this tool became the foundation I use to refine individual Marines today.

It has not let me down, nor do I expect it ever will. I am able to mold minds using this leadership tool. With it, you will be able to do the same.

◁◇▷

<◇> Chapter Seven <◇>

The Six Troop-leading Procedures

◄◊► Chapter Seven ◄◊►
The Six Troop-leading Procedures

A virtue all Marines share that rarely gets recognized is their sense of urgency. In a combat situation, delayed reaction can be the difference between life and death. In the business world, the delayed actions of a company can be disastrous. The inability to quickly adapt to changes in the marketplace can put a company out of business. Though business leaders understand the true urgency of things, it is vital that this be relayed to his/her employees. Being trained properly by a tactical strategy such as the Six Troop-leading Procedures allows a Marine to react with a sense of urgency so his/her own life can be saved or the life of the Marine to the left or right. And these Procedures can make the difference, in the business world, between a business that becomes another statistic of failure or an enormous success.

All too often, employees have a disconnected "understanding" of business. They feel that whether they make mistakes, do things slowly, poorly or without zest and pride, they will still get their paycheck at the end of the week, and the week after that. But these individuals, who are a majority, are very wrong. The condition of a business is the direct result of each person's performance. An attitude like, "someone else will handle it," for instance, is immeasurably harmful. Still, a group bullied or forced into high production would be the lowest on the chart of idealism, if such a chart were to exist. At the top of this chart would be getting agreement through understanding. The first scenario, which is sadly more common, approaches slavery, while the latter comprises free individuals with the ability to proceed with passion. Accordingly, the first never succeeds in the long-run while the ideal scene mentioned produces super-workers, gung-ho team members, and excellent leaders. What more could you ask for?

In the Corps, procrastination can ultimately give the momentum of the situation over to the enemy. The same goes for competing businesses. Simply put, the team with the greatest drive and urgency to accomplish their objectives is the ultimate winner. A sense of urgency is a trait driven into the psyche of recruits to eliminate procrastination. It increases the survival potential of each individual and thus the team as a whole. Nothing is ever a joke, nothing—even the smaller action—is ever unimportant, because all actions done well and with urgency equate to success, survival, prosperity.

The secret behind urgency is prioritization. Marines are taught to prioritize and accomplish the most important missions first. Then they evaluate the time restraints and what details must be met before they can move on.

This is a good model for you to follow as a leader. It surely aids no one to wait, waste time, and/or take numerous false steps toward the assigned goal once it is clearly defined. All that does is make it seem as if you're not an effective leader and your people don't know their jobs. That's the superficial perspective. Then there's the reality of mediocrity or worse, ultimate failure.

When a company is unable to quickly adapt to a constantly changing environment, it can kill or cripple itself. Recessions, changes in customer behavior, fads, new or growing competition... business history is filled with examples of companies that did not react fast enough, with enough forceful intention, with any sense of urgency, to an imminent threat. Logic dictates that you do not want to be part of the reason that a company failed or suffered a disastrous outcome. Reputations and successful careers are rarely built on failure.

Marines start their mission as soon as they are directed. Your team should too. In the Corps, the acronym BAMCIS is used to identify the steps necessary to make sure that a team is ready to go at a moment's notice. (The military loves acronyms because it sets an easy-to-remember structure to refer to important concepts.) You can use the same acronym to run through the preparations you need to get your group up to moving with enthusiasm and readiness as a normal operating basis, toward the desired established goals.

BAMCIS stands for:

BEGIN THE PLANNING

Once the task is given begin your plan and be detailed. If you are over-tasked, delegate authority—but not responsibility—to the person or people best suited to handle it. This way, nothing waits stagnant but instead gets done quickly.

ARRANGE FOR RECONNAISSANCE

This is another way of making you become aware of what the task is going to require. This is a critical step and is accomplished by researching what is needed in order to accomplish the task. (In the Corps, this is a vital step. As a leader you need to know what you are sending your squad up against. It's the same in business.) Either set time yourself of have someone ready to research all aspects of what you are about to undertake. If it is a marketing campaign, you're going to need to know everything about your product or service, your competition's product/service, realize who the audience is, what the time constraints are and so forth. If the task at hand is setting up a new satellite office, you will need to prepare to find out about the area: the laws, restrictions, advantage points, the people who live there, what ideal locations are available, what would make a poor location in comparison to a great one, what competition is there, what are they doing to drum up business...and so on. In short, you need to know what you're stepping into before taking a single step, so prepare for exceptional investigation of what you're about to undertake.

MAKE RECONNAISSANCE

Now actually gather all of the information through research and review it, discard what you don't need and concentrate on what is pertinent and valuable. Then formulate your plan of how to best accomplish the goal at hand. Remember, information is power. And with it, you gain the ability to predetermine things, predict most outcomes and potentialities, foresee the possibilities and know what to do before you even get to where you are going.

Adding logistics into this mission preparation phase is also a good idea. Have any supplies ready for use so you do not interrupt the process. A mechanic, for instance, would do well to first organize his tool box before starting to work on an engine. Any tools needed that were not on hand would be acquired. This type of coordination would help him do a more efficient, safer, stress-free job of it.

COMPLETE THE PLANNING

Based on the information you now have, mock up your plan of operation to fulfill the desired goal. Look over those plans and double-check the details. Have others check it as well, if appropriate, to provide for peace of mind that something has not been overlooked. To paraphrase an old saying: "Two eyes are better than one."

With good reconnaissance, you will be able to devise the ideal approach to your endeavor. Did you consider time and money constraints? Does your plan parallel with management's intentions? Will each step work out in the real world as it does on paper? Plan what is realistic, not what is wonderful, glorious, or never been done before. You can set individual targets to your team members that are under record time, but in planning, you must be realistic – always. If you have the luxury of time, include room for Murphy's Law – the unexpected, the "what can happen will happen" scenarios. You don't, and should not, put those negative potentialities in the minds of anyone else on your team; that would be counter-productive. But you yourself need to be aware and ready for any and all possibilities whether they materialize or not. That is good planning.

ISSUE THE ORDER

This means to simply assign the tasks needed to accomplish your mission from the plan you just developed. If you were driving a car, this would be the time to turn the ignition key and put the pedal to the metal. Give the orders and get everyone into action – with urgency!

SUPERVISE

One of the most important steps in this whole process is to actively supervise the task as it moves forward. Oversee what needs to be done according to the plan, but do not do it yourself. Instruct what needs to be done and provide insight if necessary. Be proactive and not reactive. This is where you utilize all of the leadership techniques and methods we have previously discussed.

This is "game on," the real thing; all of the preliminaries are over and commitment to the plan must be taken.

By simplifying what needs to be done by way of the acronym BAMCIS, it can help you with every task you assign. Running through the BAMCIS checklist before launching your team on a task means that you will not leave anything out of the steps leading up to beginning your mission. If you train yourself to operate this way you will be less likely to let details slip through the cracks, and you will succeed many times more than you will fail.

Completing every task in a timely fashion is a necessity in the Corps. There simply isn't time to waste dawdling around. It's the same in the business professional's world. Time is money. Even more important than that cliché is, "speed is power." This equates out to mean that the faster your team gets things done – with quality in mind – the more results will be accomplished. And the more results accomplished means greater survival, greater success. Just like the faster punches and escaping darts of a boxer allows him/her to win the fight, so too will you beat the competition, or enemy, with speed and adroitness. Speed is power! The leader who doesn't waste time is the one who shines.

How well I remember a particular Private First Class who had the heart of a lion and the tenacity of a pit bull. He lived for self-improvement and fierce professionalism. When he first came to my unit he was very well-rounded and had unlimited potential. This lad performed well on any task assigned to him and needed little to no supervision on completing a task.

His only problem was he lacked the experience to coordinate his explosive energy and motivation. In order to help him perform at his peak I implemented a program that forced him to use the Six Troop-leading Procedures without him even being aware of it.

I issued an order to him to have his fire team (a four-man rifle team) clean the barracks. In order for him to exercise his planning process I allowed him to review the layout of the rooms. Next, he was given a time limit to select the supplies he would need for the task. He then had to gather his cleaning gear and meet with the rest of his men so that he could issue orders and instruct them as to how they would clean the barracks. Finally, and most importantly, he was instructed to supervise his team and was given a time when I would come by and inspect.

He and his team accomplished their mission. This easy task of cleaning the barracks was a great opportunity to execute the Six Troop-leading Steps. I showed him how those six steps could apply to anything from cleaning the barracks to combat.

The lesson took hold and that Marine left with a new-found appreciation and understanding of how the Six Troop-leading Steps could be used. You can do the same in the business world. Seek out situations in which you can use these six steps, then show your team leaders how they can be applicable to numerous situations. Before you know it you will hopefully find your team using these steps automatically. Don't forget that the mark of a good leader is showing your team the way and then stepping aside...not doing things for them.

Having a sense of urgency will filter down to your team and make them aware that the task *must* be completed with all possible speed. You may or may not need to explain why there is urgency. If you're not seeing it, explain why it needs to exist. Company ABC is surpassing us, we're in a recession and need to pay the phone bill before they turn off the service, we're going for being the #1 company this year..., whatever you use to explain why, there *must be urgency* or your team or company will not keep up with the changes in the environment, inflation, the expansion of life, the daily oppression, the competition, the enemy.... Things will be sluggish. Sluggish things tend to slow down. A fast pace seems to breed more speed in all its excitement and power.

Lead your team by providing them with timelines. Praise them when they meet expectations. Be realistic and always demonstrate by example. If someone fails to meet timelines, you can provide guidance during a counseling session and instruct them to develop a better sense of urgency. Elaborate on expectations and ways to increase performance. Remind them why they need to meet timelines. Life has at times been referred to as a game, but it is certainly important to realize that it is a full-contact affair, with no one – especially the competition and the enemy – pulling any punches. Reiterate that every action is important. Help your team members streamline their goals. Remember that as a leader it is your responsibility to set them up for success. What's beautiful about all of this win-win is, ultimately, their success is your own.

‹◊› Chapter Eight ‹◊›

Mission Accomplishment: Tools to Increase Productivity

◂◈▸ Chapter Eight ◂◈▸
Mission Accomplishment:
Tools to Increase Productivity

*W*hat are the objectives of leadership? What are the ultimate goals that you, as the leader, should strive toward? There is of course the goal of meeting your immediate objective, whatever that may be. But there is more. This chapter will help you realize that and enable you to see the "big picture."

We've kept the objectives of leadership until last because people tend to operate backwards. It just seems to be better assimilated this way. First we try to implement things such as traits and principles to help us accomplish missions, without considering the role that leadership plays. But by doing things this way it imposes limits on us and our teammates. However, when you apply leadership characteristics first, as we have done in this book, mission accomplishment and team member welfare occur hand-in-hand according to plan, as a result of professional behavior. The result is true Mission Accomplishment; not just completing a task for the sake of getting it done, but accomplishing it in a style and manner that merits admiration and praise for you and your team members.

Effective leadership is exciting and energizing to everyone who works with a motivator. Everyone prospers under effective leadership. The work no longer seems like a dull chore; as each member of the team contributes, accomplishing the mission, reaching the goal unfolds as neatly as a silken tablecloth on Thanksgiving.

A good leader can be placed in any situation and find ways to improve everyone's life. From politics, academics, family relations, and work environments, to any social event, leaders have the ability to inspire. What good is inspiration without guidelines? Wouldn't team members drift around aimlessly without the leader understanding the objectives that are needed? The answer is of course yes, and thus the two objectives of good leadership are:

1. Mission Accomplishment

2. Troop Welfare

Troop welfare is a long process, and will be covered in the next chapter. Let's be concerned with Mission Accomplishment at this point.

MISSION ACCOMPLISHMENT

The first objective of good leadership is accomplishing the mission. Marines pride themselves on Mission Accomplishment. Nothing is more important to them than completing their task. Having a "can-do" attitude is etched into the mind of every Marine. Marines have accomplished incredible things throughout their existence – all because of good leadership that gives the Marines the tools and techniques to succeed. From being outnumbered and outmanned to going against unthinkable odds, history has shown that Marines are resourceful, they are relentlessly effective, and victorious...and a great deal of that has to do with leadership preparing them to accomplish their missions.

The key to Mission Accomplishment is the organization and breakdown of each individual's role in your team. If every person understands their role and gives 100 percent to accomplish the mission, it spreads the workload evenly among the team and makes every task possible and able to be accomplished.

The team members must be trained and guided and you, as the leader, must exercise your leadership skills for this to happen. Simply barking out orders and telling people what to do will not achieve the desired results. In this manner, the results that can be achieved are barely acceptable at best. And worst of all, you would set yourself and your team up for the same type of results over and over again. That's leadership? A sub-par result delivered by sub-par performances guided by sub-par effort? Any logical person would disagree and see this, at best, as mediocrity.

Look at your departments. Who are the department heads? What is their direction and intention? What are their goal(s)? Do they show through action that they know their goal(s)? To what personnel have they been assigned? Do you know who they have working for them? Knowing the answers to these questions prevents you from being what we call in the Marine Corps a Tool. The Tool is someone who wants respect but has not done anything to earn it. Don't be a Tool. Strive to be better. Ask yourself whether your department heads have the ability to answer the above questions. We have found in the Marine Corps that the chain of command is an effective process when streamlining the flow of communication. It works the same in the professional business world as well.

Breaking down each section of your company even further can increase Mission Accomplishment, because then you can have the chain of command working on the same page from virtually everywhere. This allows one supervisor to issue all instructions for a particular task. You've heard the saying about "too many cooks spoiling the broth"? This is certainly true for a mission in the Corps. How successful would it be if many different officers shouted out orders for one particular assignment? They would invariably overlap and conflict, ultimately resulting in disaster. The same is true in the business world.

For example: Middle management (in the Corps, it's the Non-Commissioned Officers) is responsible for the daily business, individual training, and development of future leaders. Higher level management (Commissioned Officers) is responsible for issuing commands, establishing policy, unit operation and effectiveness, and standards of performance and training.

Assigning team members to tasks outside of their capabilities can create extra tension in the team, and for you specifically. Before employees begin, there should be an understanding of what is required from each one of them, including the relation of their position within the levels of power and responsibility. In other words, how they fit in the overall scheme of things. This way they will be situated properly within the chain of command. One way to do this is by providing them with an initial counseling of expectations. Cover the details of the job, how to accomplish it, and when they will be reviewed on their progress. An excellent way to do this is to use a Marine Corps technique called visualization.

VISUALIZATION

Every great building is built from a vision. Your leadership is built in the same way. When Marines receive an order to carry out a mission they stand around a terrain model. A terrain model is a geographical representation of the area in which the mission is going to take place. The leader walks them through the game plan and depicts the scheme of maneuver and plan of attack as he instructs the group step-by-step.

This is known as visualization, and it is a critical tool that the Marine Corps uses to be so successful. Visualizing what must be accomplished and giving a guideline of how to accomplish the mission ensures every team member understands the role they play.

Visualization can work the same way for your team. Guide them by giving a visual demonstration of the task to be performed. Try giving a PowerPoint presentation or composing a flow chart that shows how the steps of the task logically flow into each other and who is in charge of what. Perhaps you can even work up an old-fashioned series of charts on dry-erase boards. These are gold in the Corps. (It may be low-tech, but as long as it works...) There are more ways to help your teammates visualize the goal you all must reach. After the order is given to begin, each individual department head should take his or her portion of the task and give a visual summary of expectations to their team. Once completed down to the lowest level, have every member back-brief the plan to the person they are to report things to. This way you can be assured that everything is understood.

The Marine Corps is not the only organization that uses visualization. Olympic athletes are trained to mentally visualize themselves in competition from start to finish. All actions start with thought, and the mind's eye has the ability to manifest all actions. Put visualization to work for you. At the next employees meeting, use a visualization tool, such as PowerPoint. Make sure that when you do so, the visual demonstration includes the inner vision to understand the direction of the company and the overall command levels. Let them see the race and then the victory before the sound of the gun. Search for ways to map out success in your mind before the mission starts, and then share them with your team.

Here's an example of how visualization can work.

In July of 1998, Kilo Company 3rd Battalion 6th Marines held a fire team competition. This competition consisted of sixteen fire teams battling it out in six different events, such as a military obstacle course, disassembly and assembly of various infantry weapons, a physical fitness test, etc.

Before the competition started I asked the team to point out any of our collective weak points. They all had concerns, so I opted to break away from the rest of the teams in order to find a quiet place to focus their minds. Then I instructed them to see themselves performing in each event, see how flawless the run down the obstacle course would be as we relayed to the front. We practiced disassembling the M-16 A2 service rifle in our imaginations and raced to put it back together. Each member had to focus on completing these tasks in order to be the winner.

As the competition started we streaked through the events. I wanted to keep this momentum so before we would start the next challenge we would all focus on hitting each obstacle with precision and grace while maintaining dominance as the leaders.

At the end of the competition we were victorious and the Company acknowledged our hard work. It felt good to win but felt even better to exercise the winning mindset. Executing flawlessly starts in the mind and is part of a bigger picture.

COMMANDER'S INTENT

When something needs to get done, orders are given. Those orders, in the Marines, are known as the

Commander's Intent.

The Commander's Intent is the basic goal or objective of the mission statement. It establishes the way a team member is supposed to behave, it defines what to do, it determines how things will be accomplished, and provides the means to a specific end. The Commander's Intent is broken down so that the lowest levels of leadership can understand and follow it. The purpose is for the most senior person to clearly state the goal. It is the guiding element that removes the possibility for misunderstandings or ambiguity. When the plan hits friction points, team members can remain stable, on track, and not lose sight of their direction in achieving the Commander's Intent and the current mission.

When an order is given, there are many moving parts that need to move in unison in order to achieve the desired results. Almost always in combat, the original plans change due to unforeseen circumstances. These can range from an unexpected enemy force showing up or coming from an unpredicted position to a flat tire on a vehicle. Something as simple as a flat tire can affect numerous things, such as the duration of the mission or its time of completion. In turn, these unforeseen incidents open the door for yet more unexpected changes.

One of the most important aspects of the Commander's Intent is empowerment. The intention is to lead without constraint or restriction that could cause the mission to fail or result in unnecessary impairment to it. It is all about delegating appropriate degrees of power to each of the subordinate command/management levels

Not only does empowerment grant the power of decision, it also assigns the responsibility where it should lie – with the people who have been assigned to accomplish a task. Otherwise, in an autonomous leadership environment, one can rightfully say in defense of failure that he or she was just following orders. One also has to consider the ramifications of command exterior to ground zero. It is usually difficult, if not impossible, to adequately make quick adjudications when not knowing the exact circumstances of the event. Often, immediate decision from witnessing eyes is required in order to make the best choice for the mission at hand.

So the Commander's Intent says what needs to be done and gives details on how it is to be executed—*if* there are no collisions with opposition or the unexpected. If that should occur, then a leader must use good judgment and change the tactical plan. For instance, during an operations order I was instructed by my commander to go into an area to make some observations. Upon entering the area I discovered that the view was obstructed. I used my own tactical plan to move to a hilltop that could provide a better field of view and still complete the mission. My job was first and foremost to complete the task, not to robotically or mindlessly do exactly the actions given, "no matter what."

Leaders need to operate independently and be able to demonstrate their ability to lead. Overall objectives, such as the Commander's Intent, provide the guidelines under which to operate. This approach creates a will to perform and increases the eagerness to proactively demonstrate Situational Awareness. In other words, it provides a cognizance and understanding of the existing scene in all its aspects. It is critical to communicate clearly, concisely, and as simply as possible so the plan can be understood by each member of the team. When the intent is understood by each Marine, the commander receives the power of Marines doing their jobs on their own initiatives.

There are no limits to human ability. We have walked on the moon and split the atom. Humans are capable of unleashing tremendous problem-solving capability to eliminate situations as they arise. Supercharge your team members with the basic overall goal, communicate it in as simple terms as needed for success, and watch your group respond. Setting forth the Commander's Intent is one of the most important aspects of Marine leadership. Few people outside the Corps know about this simple but critical tool for becoming an effective leader. Now you know it too.

Now perhaps you can see the big picture – how this all fits together. The tasks come from the plan of the day. The plan of the day comes from the weekly training schedule and the weekly training schedule comes from the Commander's Intent.

In the Marines, the entire chain of command plays a role in order for the company to successfully complete its mission. Each individual link plays a role in Mission Accomplishment. In the business world, the same is true;

everyone, from the highest level executive to the lowest ranked team member, is responsible for the goal to be reached.

Investing in leadership and morale management is simple. The dividends, as I hope you can see by now, are spectacular.

‹◊› Chapter Nine ‹◊›

Team Member Welfare: Taking Care of Your Greatest Investment

‹◊› Chapter Nine ‹◊›
Team Member Welfare: Taking Care of Your Greatest Investment

*O*n occasion I like to start a speaking engagement about leadership with a specific attention-gainer. I ask the members of the audience to perform an exercise that was developed to increase self-awareness. "Take out a piece of paper and write down the name of your favorite leader. Think about it for a second.... It could be a family member such as your mother or father or it could be a politician. It doesn't matter who it is as long as you are familiar with them. Now jot down some of the things they have done to inspire you to be a better person. It can range from things like providing food on the table to fighting for Civil Rights. Make it a detailed list and look at what you wrote down."

The majority of people who honestly complete this survey find themselves honoring their parents for all the long hard work they have put in for them. This is the fundamental of this chapter. Looking after the welfare of your team is much like a parent looking after the welfare of a child. Remember, A LEADER PROVIDES!

The welfare of your team members is a melting pot of combined characteristics. As leader, it is your responsibility to try to keep your team members happy, focused, and in accord. Marine Corps leaders have quickly found out how difficult – if not impossible – it is to try and achieve an objective with a distracted, squabbling team. The same is true for the business world. All hands in the lifeboat must pull together or the boat meanders aimlessly. In this chapter we will discuss such things as providing, authority, responsibility, accountability, customs, morale, and other tools for you to use to enhance Team Member Welfare.

Unfortunately, sometimes disciplinary action is the required form of leadership and the best type of team welfare you can apply. Even if your team members are not happy, the integrity of the circumstances should dictate the consequence. Employee welfare requires impeccable integrity and courage.

The motto "semper fidelis" in the Marine Corps means "always faithful." These words are etched onto the hearts of every Marine. Marines group together outside of their element like a pack of wolves. They have each other as guardian angels in combat and on liberty in town. A Marine is made to realize that watching the backs of the Marine to the left and right of him or her is an honor. To be part of a culture that focuses on Honor, Courage, and Commitment is unexplainable, and fosters a bond that is unbreakable. You can do the same with your team members, and form that same kind of bond. Unlocking the human potential is what the Corps excels at, and is what this book is striving to do for you. Allowing your team members to reach "Mission Accomplishment" is Team Member Welfare. Allow them the opportunity to be proud.

What does Team Member Welfare mean? There is no one answer. For example, more than just checking on the safety of an individual, it could mean placing that individual outside their comfort zone to prepare them for advancement. Remember that the easiest way to judge a leader is to look at his/her team. If the team is motivated then they have a motivated leader in you. Simply put, the team reflects the inner core of their leader.

There are many ways to ensure Team Member Welfare:

- **PROVIDING** — This is the main thing that a good leader can do: **provide** for one's team. Ask yourself what you can provide and what the impact of delivering it would be to a team member in need? Providing cannot be measured because circumstances dictate the significance of the need and how important it is to the individual. But know this: Providing is the ultimate display of team welfare.

Some of the many things a leader can provide are:

- **SOLUTIONS** — You need to be a problem solver.

- **ANSWERS** — People look to you and your position for the answer. If you don't know the answer, they are confident that you will know where to find it.

- **GUIDANCE** — You can show a team member the best way to accomplish their task by using your education, experience, or a combination of the two.

- **ENCOURAGEMENT** – Just as my colleague author, Robert, states in his literary services company's slogan, "Never underestimate the power of good communication.™," words are a powerful tool to transmit thought from one person to another. Use your words to motivate and build confidence and trust.

  Realize that thought is king. It can make or break someone because what someone "believes" is what they "are." Words are not just a combination of letters or only representations of things. Words have meaning, and what they mean affects people. Chew someone out, cut them down, tell them they are nothing..., and eventually they will come to believe this to be the case. However, if you compliment, encourage, show them how truly great they are at something, you will empower them with immeasurable personal strength and well-being. Their physical health will even be visibly affected.

- **DISCIPLINE** — Accountability enables people to know where the limits lie. Rules, laws, principles, mores exist for the purpose of the viability of the team, group, society.... Making these established acceptable forms of behavior known enables, 1) agreement and 2) understanding of the consequences if one were to transgress them. This allows for your team members to use good sound logic in their decisions, based on personal ethics. For all intents and purposes, discipline eliminates the need for justice action. It also gives a sense of comfort and calm that only good control and boundaries can supply a group.

- **INSIGHT** – This refers to the ability to see complex things clearly, intuitively, as they really are. Giving insight to someone means to give them the ability to understand and find solutions to his or her personal problems. How can a person fix problem behavior if they don't see it or know what it is? You must bring insight (awareness, perceptiveness) to a group to identify and rectify problem behavior.

- **THE STANDARD** — By example and by explanation, show the level of excellence that is expected and acceptable. Interestingly enough, you might think at first that The Standard might be the absolute very best, perfection. But this in many cases would not be realistic nor practical. The Standard could be different from company to company or mission to mission. If your team produced a disposable product that

147

was designed to earn profits through large volumes of sales, then quality and excellence, like you might find in Swiss watches, would not be the correct level of quality. In the case of producing disposable cigarette lighters, for instance, The Standard might be the number of working lighters produced per hour, not a perfectly-built lighter.

Someone not knowing The Standard would be certain to get it wrong and possibly come off as being defiant or a poor worker. Letting your team know the level of competence, quality and speed will protect them from unnecessary toil and/or failure.

- **ACKNOWLEDGMENT** — People want their hard work to be recognized. You are the one who must do that before anyone else. The value in a comment, or write-up, of a job well done cannot be overestimated.

- **ABILITY** — Give your team members the tools of information, education, drilling, and training to succeed and they will use them to everyone's benefit. Confidence grows out of ability. A confident team able to perform their tasks adroitly is the ideal arrangement a leader could ever aspire to create.

These are just some of the many things a leader can provide. Certainly there are others that can be conjured. Take the time to develop other provisions that will help the welfare of your team(s). Providing is important because it creates a connection between upper and lower levels of management, and over time grows into a solid bond of trust. This helps everyone to contribute even more.

Authority

Authority, more than anything, is the "privilege" to oversee assignments and direct the team toward standards by tasking subordinates. Never confuse authority with leadership, as they are distinctly different. Authority stems from what has to be done while leadership is the way you go about getting it done. Your authority over anyone is to a great degree an illusion and superficial. People work for you for many different reasons. Do they respect you as a person or do they respect your billet, job description, rank, or a combination of all?

Your scope of authority ranges from one position to the next. As a leader you have a responsibility to be strong-willed. Sometimes, workers take advantage of management and it creates a lackadaisical environment. This does not mean that you should be a dictator, but rather stand up for organizational policies and procedures and hold people to the standard those guidelines establish. Say what you mean, and mean what you say. Having authority is an honor and your focus should be to guide the team without hesitation to achieve the best results in the quickest timeframe—not to flaunt your authority, play cat and mouse, pay favors, or play favoritism.

We've all known managers who take their position of authority and take on a false importance of themselves and think they are a gift that graced the people they work for. These managers yell and point fingers at everyone all day long to demonstrate that they are a leader. The term "power play" means to "make" people do things unnecessary just to show one's power over people. If someone refuses, they're fired on the spot as an example of what will happen to the rest if they dare try such mutiny. They give no acknowledgement for successful projects, acting like there was failure. They only bring up the bad, and play down the good that people do. They act like, or boast openly that things would be a total failure without them and the team means nothing and has no worth. They take undue credit and never take responsibility for failures – "it's the team's fault!" This type of behavior only creates barriers. No one on the team is ever fooled by such campaigns. This type gets no respect and things "happen" here and there, like things breaking down and problems popping up "out of the blue."

Critiquing is a fundamental technique, but the manner in which you demonstrate your authority should be out of respect – never vainglorious self-promotion. Take a moment to reflect on your authority behavior. How do you go about your whole leadership style? Are you an authoritarian dictator or do you show personal strength by being able to bare humility and respect? See if there is any way you might be able to get greater respect and agreement. Remember, respect can never be demanded. It can only be earned.

Responsibility and Accountability

In the Marine Corps, if you hold one person accountable for misconduct and then you fail to hold another accountable for the same misconduct, you taint team welfare with corruption. The same is true in the professional world. Rules are there for a reason and consequences must be employed in an unbiased manner. As the leader, you must hold your employees accountable as you would hold yourself.

Try this simple test to determine responsibility and accountability within your team: Ask each team member who is ultimately responsible for the team to meet its goal. Each of them should say they are. If not, you know you have work to do in the accountability department. Every team member should be held accountable.

In the Marines, seeking responsibility for your actions is a necessity for good team welfare. Shifting blame and pointing fingers only creates hostility and resentment. It is also a form of betrayal to the team. Your job as the leader is to keep friction to a minimum in the workplace.

Customs

Traditions are born through customs. Having customs distinguishes one team from the next and helps create prediction, good expectations, and familiarity within the group. Such uniqueness and qualities of foresight are positive and stabilizing benefits to the team members who have the exclusive privilege of being part of them. Devising things like awards, traditional ceremonies and events can enable your team to feel a strong sense of belonging, like they stand out, are a part of something unique and special. These things also have a way of boosting healthy competition between teammates. Honor your established customs and morale will increase among the group. Customs, courtesies, and traditions give a sense of history to the Marine Corps. It is an honor to display courtesy and have the ability to be part of centuries-old traditions. And speaking of morale...

Morale

Morale is the pulse of the people or the mass emotion that fuels the workplace. Morale management is an art unto itself. Solid leadership will raise morale and increase worker enthusiasm. How well do you really know your team's morale? Are they just telling you what you want to hear? Morale can be seen and felt. Observe what you see in your team. Is everyone moving around at a swift pace? Is that pace light-hearted or frantic? What is the overall tone of the group – Boredom? Fear? Mild Interest? Cheerful? Exhilaration? Remember, even good morale can be raised.

Never consider that work has to be serious business. This is a big mistake managers with low esteem and great incompetence think the workplace must be like. A laugh or a grin is viewed as defiance, unruliness, and nonproductive. But the most unproductive thing a leader can ever create within their teams is contempt for each other. If you're not sure if this is true, you can always take note of the speed of activity and level of mistakes at different emotional levels of your team. What will be found is that the further down scale, the more serious or saddened a group is, the slower it produces. An interesting phenomenon that happens on the way down is it begins to pick up temporary speed around the realm of anger. But as you might imagine, the results of the activity are more destructive than productive. Have you even seen an angry person take care in anything that they've done? Though things may be done swiftly, they are done without concern, carelessly, and in a destructive manner. Things "seem to" break more, and actual products completed are in no comparison of quality to those produced in higher states of, say, cheerfulness or strong interest.

Think of team members as pillars that support and hold your company up. When one pillar collapses the strain is felt on all the others. Morale can help in these matters. Employees in high morale are stronger and more supportive than those in low morale. The "pillars" (employees) that remain motivated and strong keep the company up and running. When everyone works together the load lightens for each.

Improvise, adapt, and overcome. A key to high morale is to create a flexible work environment that proactively seeks change. Unexpected change in the workplace can lead to fear and consequently a negative mind frame. Extinguish people's fears by educating them

153

on the types of change that may or may not occur. Furthermore, let them know what course of action should or would be taken if change happens. Fear of the unknown is another morale-zapper.

Enthusiasm and motivation encourage team members to do their best. When workers are motivated and morale is high work becomes fun. When a job is fun to do, normal limits are broken and everyone's focus becomes positive. This positive energy enables people to break records and destroy limitations. Imagine what could be accomplished in your company without limits! Imagine how well that would reflect on you as the leader who helped make it possible!

Morale management is underrated. The effects of morale management are long-term and easy to apply. However, one way **not** to improve morale is by ordering mandatory fun days. Mandatory fun days do not raise morale. They are a quick fix to low morale and all they do is waste a lot of time and energy. **Leadership** is the best way to raise morale. Invest in your people by understanding the dynamics of your personnel.

Again, know yourself and seek self-improvement. Examine how you have increased morale. Ask yourself what you can do as a leader to increase motivation around the workplace.

Training

When you think about the welfare of any employee

you have to think critically about their training. How well did you set each individual up for success? Did you provide the tools needed to get the job done? One major reason Marines are so successful is because of how much they train. However, more important is what they get from that training. The Marines use a leadership philosophy called "Crawl, Walk, Run." It sets individuals up for success by showing how something is done, then allowing the person to do it under supervision, and finally allowing the person to do it while the leader only supervises the results.

Do you fill your downtime with training or do you allow the time to fritter away by allowing your employees to sit idle? A training structure can be as simple or elaborate as you want it to be, or as it needs to be. It can fill a fifteen-minute period or it can take weeks or months to complete. It depends on what level of skill and ability is expected to be accomplished.

Marines are trained to know their peers' jobs and the job of their immediate supervisor as well. This sets them up for success when it's time to advance and can come in quite handy when someone moves up or out. Imagine that a department head is moving to another job with a different company. What if the two weeks' notice given was not enough time to complete a project that was under development? If the other members of the team had been trained properly then any one of them could step up to the task and complete the project.

Proper training prevents injury and provides a safe work environment. Nothing offers as much Team Member

Welfare as training. Skill and competence comes with a balance of hands-on drilling and study. Try to make training as interesting as possible. A lot of civilian training is done by an overload of lecture and has a tendency to be boring. Incorporate different approaches to training to make it challenging, appealing, and fun. Hold competitions and group discussions during your training block so that they break up the monotony of the day. This way the class can willingly focus on the importance of what is being taught. Remember that your goal is to have learning become a result and not a focus.

Don't fall into a common trap: Most training is the result of mandatory topics that need to be covered before an employee starts a job. The training begins and ends there, and the employee receives only minimum requirements throughout the year. But even before this, the essence and purpose of training is completely missing from these lifeless approaches to employee training. Give them sound reasons to want to train instead of "because you have to," or "it's part of staff requirements." If there are incentives, like advancement in position or pay for competence, or other such motivations, make these known to your team. Enabling someone to choose to do something versus "having no choice" makes an enormous difference in attitude and how one applies him/herself, and this includes training.

Once you've got their interest raised for getting trained, then you can think up and add more concepts to include in their training – data that will best help them to really succeed. Take a look at what might give them an edge in what they do. Ask yourself: What brings in the most money for the company? What is the big ticket item that you have? Shouldn't that be covered in training as well? Think further outside the box. Why does the training have to stop there?

Empower your team members. Find time to educate your people. Education is an important component of team welfare.

Standards

When thinking about the welfare of employees, standards might be the last thing to cross one's mind. Most employees feel pressure to reach the standards listed in the policies and procedures of most companies. Surveys show that employees have a negative perception about standards because the methods used to make corrections to bring someone to a certain standard can seem to be negative, degrading and/or even disciplinary.

Setting standards helps improve anyone who strives to meet higher levels of achievement. It's a fact that the path of least resistance is very tempting and often heeded. Leaving each member to figure out their own productivity goals can often be fruitless. Therefore, setting standards at appropriate and realistic levels—high enough for difficult attainment, but not unreachable—causes people to go further than they "thought" they could. Standards force people out of their comfort zone and make them reach, adapt, expand as individuals. Holding people accountable is crucial for the standards to have an effect. Just the important, reward has to be part of the equation for high achievers.

Marines are held to standards in many areas other than job performance. For instance, Grooming Standards grade Marines on personal appearance. A clean-shaven face and squared-away uniform not only represent the Marine Corps in good fashion, but will also display the attention to detail that the individual Marine possesses. In turn, the Marine adopts the grooming standard as his or her own and then strives to achieve it in other situations in his/her life.

Leaders should enforce standards and have the situational awareness to make corrections on a continual basis. This will ensure all-around discipline of the unit and breed high standards between colleagues over time. A team led by a good leader seldom requires upper levels of leadership to correct violations. Team tolerance levels as a whole dwindle with increased perfection, discipline and pride. And low standards are met with peer pressure of the best kind. In other words, team members will demand that any sluggards come up to the standard of the group. A well organized and disciplined team creates a highly functional and safe work environment.

Again, know yourself and seek self-improvement. Have you ever overlooked a standard intentionally? Do you hold others to a different standard than yourself? What can you do to maintain the highest standards for your team?

Self-discipline

There is much to lose when Marines are on the line, doing their jobs. They don't stand to lose million dollar deals, important clients, or blunder away investment opportunities. They risk life and limb. Self-discipline is critical to all jobs and situations. Too much can go wrong without it. Team welfare depends on one and all to not fall asleep at their posts, remain mentally alert, and have the endurance needed to keep their fellow Marines alive.

Metaphorically speaking, each team member of your company keeps the company alive. Instilling self-discipline and having people hold themselves to the highest standard is the sign of a healthy organization. One of the obvious ways to reach a standard is through implementing Quality Assurance by having others exterior to the activity check the work of the activity. But through each individual's personal attention to detail and self-discipline within the group itself, you take QA, and the standard, to a whole new level.

Individuals who lack self-discipline can be motivated in many ways. Counseling, discussion, and example are three ways that self-discipline can be increased. Through these means, the willingness grows. Another way is by upholding the company's standards and operating according to its policies and procedures. Don't be fooled by the complaints of a few about control. Good control is something that the majority of people appreciate. Knowing one is in the hands of a good group or company is comforting. It's about longevity and surviving well on a

159

day-to-day basis. And when someone has good self-discipline, they feel better about themselves. Instilling self-discipline is without question Team Member Welfare.

Confidence

As a leader, having confidence in yourself is a big step in Team Member Welfare. Let your employees believe in you and it will set them at ease. Do not create a self-fulfilling prophecy by trying to sell an idea you aren't confident about. Take care of second-guessing and fear of failure quickly. People know when something feels good and they also understand when something feels wrong. Set yourself at ease and others will follow your lead.

In the Marine Corps, confidence is a key element to success. Not too many missions would be successful if the Marines going into them were plagued by doubt. They would panic and quit at the first sign of adversity. But they never have, and they never will, because they have the strength that supreme confidence instills.

Display belief in yourself and others will naturally assume belief in you as well. Let your actions indicate your motives. You do not need to explain yourself. Leaders explain the plan, not themselves. Trust in your ability to lead and know your cause is just. Your character will become the model for both the experienced and the young. Confidence and motivation work together to energize your team members. When a team's leader has it, confidence is imbued in his/her team members.

Communication

How can Team Member Welfare occur if people cannot understand the person in charge? Think about the ramifications of this. If you are consistently misinterpreted and your team thinks they are doing what you desire but in reality they are way off base, how can the outcome possibly achieve the desired result? Accurate communication is critical to ensure mission accomplishment and Team Member Welfare.

Watch a Marine communicate: it is almost as if he or she is speaking another language. Simple and confident, a Marine says what he means and means what he says. The message here is obvious. Too many times in business the central message is obscure or abstruse. The result is a serious amount of wasted time and money, and frustrated employees who thought they were doing what was required. You should explain and elaborate in a clear and concise manner. Drive home only necessary and important points in the simplest of terms. Realize that it is not just your communication to consider but also the duplication by the recipients.

To pave the way for clear communication, organize your thoughts and visualize how you will present your material. Have a key point, then elaborate briefly on it. Remember that simplicity is priceless in any explanation. Stay to your structure and avoid tangents – unless they exemplify your point. If you find yourself off topic lead the conversation back to what is important. Lead your people with the ability to convey your intent. Stay to the body of your discussion. Once the points have been made, summarize and have your team members back-brief to ensure their understanding of your intent.

Miscommunication and misunderstanding are common disasters in business, yet they don't have to be. Before you communicate try to break the topic down so that it can be understood by anyone. Research your topic and listen to yourself from the point of view of your team. Try to troubleshoot any possible misinterpretations before you brief your people on what needs to be covered. Simply planning your dialogue will aid in reducing misinterpretations.

NEVER assume that anyone knows what you're talking about. In other words, don't take the present knowledge and understanding of your team members for granted. Quite often, people have confusions about things but have never gotten the nerve to ask or learn more about them. Visualize what it is they need to know fundamentally in order to grasp what you will be telling them in your next briefing. Then either quickly explain those fundamentals, which can often not be a practical thing to do, or keep in mind those basics. And if you run into a bunch of glassy-eyed people, some who have nodded off, know that they have missed something – likely the fundamentals are not understood – and things must be clarified. During the back-brief, you can ask questions or request examples or demonstrations about the different concepts to make sure that they really have duplicated your information.

There is another aspect of communication that leaders often tend to overlook. It is equally as important as speaking: listening. Listening can save your organization time and money. If a team member has a better way of doing something, why would you not want to hear about it and then employ it? Reflective listening is the ability to listen to what has been said, internalize the information and then say it back. It is critical in the Marines, and should be for you as well. Every leader should train themselves as well as their teammates to use reflective listening. You could be the best public speaker ever, but if the intended group is the worst of listeners, your communication is going to be ineffective. Effective communication requires both speaker and listener to simply try to understand the information passed between them. Don't talk *at* your audience as if it were a wall. Make sure that you want to talk and they want to listen. Any lacking in either will be a serious breakdown of communication, not to mention a waste of time. Look at the results you are causing in your listeners. Are they attentive, highly interested, bright-eyed? When you ask a question do they respond indifferently or with eagerness?

There is so much importance riding on communication. It is the thread that connects everyone together. Does your group have good communication or otherwise? It is your responsibility to ensure that your team members duplicate your message. ◄◊►

‹◊› Chapter Ten ‹◊›

Bringing It All Together: Using Each Concept to Refine Your Leadership Skills

‹◊› Chapter Ten ‹◊›

Bringing It All Together: Using Each Concept to Refine Your Leadership Skills

*T*he perfect leader is a myth. There is no such thing. No one has all the answers, but trying our best to lead through integrity and humility will set our own hearts and minds at ease. The opinions of others come from flawed perceptions; they are not experiencing the same dynamics as you. There will be times to listen and learn from them but also times to disregard them because of the self-glorification that most people have. Believe in yourself and the direction you want your team to go. Let your understanding unlock the way.

It is impossible to perfectly learn everything that goes into leadership. Take what you can learn from others who have succeeded with it, as from this book and others like it, and continue to realize for yourself as much greatness and perfection as you possibly can. All you can do is direct yourself to personal growth. Make yourself a better person and it will make better people of those who surround you. Learn what to do as well as what not to do. Focus your attention on how to lead and forgive yourself for any mistakes.

When I was promoted to Corporal and given a Rifle Squad of twelve men, it was one of the greatest moments of my life. Being a small unit leader of Marines is a dream come true and I had won in a board against the best in the Battalion to earn my spot amongst the others.

In those early days it was a crucible of trial and error in forging my leadership approaches. On a hot summer day I marched my squad to an open field where I could give a class on patrolling and conduct some rehearsals. Not having the experience of a true professional I began my class swearing and using profanity to show how dominant I was. Little to my knowledge it made me appear to be an amateur. A Captain happened to step into the class without being noticed. His name was Captain Pfeiffer and he was my company commanding officer.

My class continued without interruption until it was finished. Then the good Captain stepped out of the crowd and pulled me to the side while the men practiced immediate action drills. He verbally counseled me on professionalism and how profanity does nothing to better your image. It was a lesson that I kicked myself over because I knew better than to lower my standards. Yet it was a great learning point because of my being immature and in truth the mistake has made me a better leader as well as a better man.

The Marine Corps would not be the elite organization it is if its leaders beat themselves up over every mistake, then second-guessed themselves till death thereafter. Mistakes are unfortunate, but people are human and do make mistakes. It's why pencils have erasers. The folly is not in making a mistake but in not learning from it. In the Corps, plenty of mistakes are made by those in leadership positions. But they learn from these mistakes and move forward, determined not to make the same mistake again. In fact, there are reports called "Lessons Learned" that come from the mistakes and success of other units. The Marines look forward, not backward. So should you. Little is gained by replaying and bemoaning a past mistake.

Remember, leadership is not about you. It is about the people you lead. It is about accomplishing and directing. We as leaders should treat people with respect by demonstrating tact and loyalty. Leadership is about giving and not what you can get from others. When you give, you get back ten-fold in human loyalty. I have seen it occur time and again in the Marine Corps, and so has my co-author, Robert, seen it in the professional business world. You will see it occur as well, but you must start the ball rolling by your actions.

Leadership has many unique aspects that can make it difficult at times. For Marines, leadership comes naturally because of the constant education and self-discipline that cycle through the career course. You do not act as a leader in the Corps—you become one. Education and constant study of the leadership arts is a primary requirement for all Marines. It is, frankly, how I have achieved the leadership role I play today.

Each topic discussed in this text is part of a puzzle. This puzzle creates a powerful picture of the goals that can be accomplished. The values and principles universally fit and blend with other traits to synergistically create a leadership style. No leadership style is wrong. There are more effective styles that can be used in certain times and situations. Having knowledge of them as well as experience and working with an open mind, aids in using the best approach and style for that moment. It is our responsibility to learn more about leadership and build an arsenal of the best approaches to implement for any scenario you might encounter. Full enlightenment does not come from the result, but from the journey.

Continuing to assess and analyze your leadership qualities will refine your skills to razor-sharp perfection. Understand that every aspect of a leader can be improved through educating yourself and others. It has been an honor to talk to you about Marine leadership. It is the primary goal of this text to increase the quality of your leadership and your life. Becoming a Marine literally saved my life. Becoming a leader of men and women was a most welcome byproduct of the Marine experience. And to helped me in my spiritual journey to change and become a better person – a better, contributing member of the human race. In this book, you have hopefully been given many opportunities to make those changes as well. With Robert Nahas' business expertise infused within the pages, it only helped my cause in ultimately sharing the effective and esoteric understandings of leadership of the Marines for the civilian world to use in order to flourish and prosper. Now it is up to you to put into effect what you have learned.

If you have any questions on any of the material we have covered, feel free to e-mail me personally at: aleaderprovides@yahoo.com . It would be an honor to help you in any way that I can.

References:

MCO 5390.2D, Leadership Training and Education

FM 22-100, Military Leadership